English
Essentials Explained

Jill Bray

How to Master
the Basics of
English Grammar,
Spelling, Punctuation
– and so much more!

English Essentials Explained – How to Master the Basics of English Grammar, Spelling, Punctuation – and so much more!

©Jill Bray

ISBN: 978-1-906316-92-1

Published in 2011 by HotHive Books, Evesham, UK.
www.thehothive.com

The right of Jill Bray to be identified as the author of this work has been asserted by her in accordance with the Copyright, Designs and Patents Act 1988.

Printed in the UK by TJ International, Padstow.

The Queen Elizabeth Hospital
King's Lynn
NHS Foundation Trust

Library/Knowledge Services
The Queen Elizabeth Hospital
Tel: 01553-613269
Email: library.services@qehkl.nhs.uk
Online: www.elms.nhs.uk
for renewal

Due for return:

Preface

Is this book for you? Do you need help with any of the following: basic written and spoken English (grammar, common errors, spelling, punctuation, style, drafting, writing, proofreading, etc.)? Do you recognise yourself here?

- You're a university, college or sixth form lecturer/teacher, who'd like to find a straightforward book to recommend to your students to enable them to write and speak English more accurately.
- You're a student who has to produce written work, and you're concerned about what kind of impression this may make. Your English grammar and usage skills may be inadequate, so you'd like to improve these quickly.
- You're a student who hasn't reached the grades you'd hoped to achieve and think that this may be partly because of your weak English. You're also apprehensive about your future job prospects and think that these would be better if your English were better.
- You've completed your formal education, but are worried that the standard of your written or spoken English may not be good enough for the challenges ahead. You may have already started a job, but your lack of a good foundation in English may hinder your promotion.
- You're a teacher of a subject other than English and are aware that your own English skills need to be more proficient in order for you to advise your students more competently.
- Your first language is not English, and you know that there are gaps in your knowledge of English grammar. You may speak English well, but you'd like to find a book which would enable you to write and speak English with more confidence.
- You're a business, company or website owner who needs to advertise on or off the Internet, but have gaps in your written English, e.g. you don't know how to start drafting a piece of written work so that the style of your finished, polished work will impress enough to generate a first-rate financial result.
- You'd like to be more confident in work and social situations and react to those around you in the way they expect of you. The times when you should use formal language, informal language and slang are covered here, so you'll be advised which to use when.
- You'd appreciate a reference book to remind you of the basics of grammar and other points connected with speaking and writing.
- You'd like to have a wider vocabulary, but don't know where to start.
- You're prepared to make the effort now in order to acquire a lifetime of invaluable knowledge. Progress is monitored at the end of each Unit (answers given).
- You're not any of the above, but you have always wanted to have *English Essentials Explained*!

This book is easy to use even if you have 'failed' in English in the past. It gives clear explanations for those with no knowledge of any particular point, yet is also comprehensive enough to stretch the brightest minds and those who would like to learn more.

Everyone needs, on occasions, to write and speak correctly, stylishly and effectively in English. With this book, you'll learn not only how to, but also how not to. Discover that English grammar, spelling, punctuation, etc. are not difficult: they just require some thought and practice.

There's always someone who will judge you by the way you write or speak. Some employers reject a CV with just one spelling mistake! I once read how a consulting engineer did just that, because, he argued, if an applicant made errors in spelling, he might be equally careless with calculations!

Many people just don't think when they start to write or speak. Don't be one of those writers whose fingers run away with them, whose thoughts are muddled, whose spelling, punctuation, grammar and style leave a lot to be desired. Read what I have to say and give it some thought.

You won't find a complete reference to everything about English grammar here. No, I've made it a lot easier for you than that: I've selected just the points that you really need to know (plus at least 30 Advanced Points). However, I suggest that you ignore the latter if you aren't very confident in English. They're included to stretch those of you who are already proficient in the English language.

Although you may not use written or spoken Standard English all or even much of the time, situations and occasions could arise when a good knowledge of this, particularly when writing, will definitely help you; so you should be prepared. [Standard English is the name of the type of formal English language used by educated people who know and apply the rules of English grammar, both in speech and in writing. This is covered fully in Unit 5.]

If you don't read much, this could put you at a disadvantage when it comes to writing. We all model ourselves on others. Writing correctly, interestingly and with a clear, accurate style is no exception. Read authors of every kind, and learn how to write from good examples. As long as you're thinking about what you read, noting its correctness and style, read whatever you like.

It's often lack of thought or a slip in concentration, rather than lack of knowledge, which causes mistakes such as 'from' for 'form' or 'you' for 'your'. So, I'll give you the knowledge, and you provide the thought. Once you get used to thinking about your English, it will become second nature – and you, like the small elephant on the cover, won't ever forget again.

We all make mistakes, and I should be very surprised if there are none in the 54,000 words of this book. However, if you study *English Essentials Explained*, you'll certainly make fewer mistakes in the future.

There's a misconception among some people, both on and off the Internet, that writing English is easy, and that all you have to do is to sit down at your computer and start. Yes, you could do it that way – but you'll do it a lot better if you study *English Essentials Explained* first and keep it by your side for handy reference. You'll find here all the tools for writing and speaking in whatever situation you find yourself.

As for books you should own, at the very least, you must have a largish dictionary and some kind of reference book on grammar. A thesaurus is very useful if you're intending to write at some length. As explained above, I have not attempted to cover everything in *English Essentials Explained*, but I trust I shall whet your appetite enough for you to buy some books yourself and to have them constantly by your side for quick and easy reference.

How to use this book

1. One suggested approach, before reading anything else, is to turn straight to **Unit 1: Review** (Page 47) and write down as many answers as you can. Note your score. Then try this Review again once you've studied the relevant Unit and answer the questions again. Continue in this way, one Unit at a time. Repeat this as many times as you wish until you feel secure.
2. A second option is to study the book a Tip at a time, moving quickly past what you already know and concentrating on points which are new to you.
3. Questions are asked throughout the text. Try to answer these without first looking at the answers (which aren't always given, as it's sometimes assumed that you're clever enough to know them!).
4. This book is designed for both study and reference. If you want to use it for reference, look through all the pages to familiarise yourself with how the book is organised, so that you can quickly find what you need.
5. Look out for the ✓ and ✗ signs. The ✓ shows a correct answer, whereas the ✗ (you've guessed it) shows one which is wrong.

To keep you awake when you should concentrate hard, you'll see ✱ by some points. Just look on ✱ as the kind of ping your computer may make, for example, when you close a document or receive an email. Or think of it as a doorbell, an alarm or anything else which grabs your attention. Then think!

User ID:	**Your name**
Password:	**Think!**

Contents

Unit 1: Grammar

"I will not go down to posterity talking bad grammar."

Disraeli, correcting proofs of his last Parliamentary speech

TIP 1 Parts of speech

Noun	Pronoun
Verb	Preposition
Adverb	Conjunction
Adjective	Interjection

Here's a sentence with all eight:
The man leaned dangerously over the low bridge and he fell into the river – splash!

Find the parts of speech you know, and then look at the analysis below:

man	noun	*and*	conjunction
leaned	verb	*he*	pronoun
dangerously	adverb	*fell*	verb
over	preposition	*into*	preposition
low	adjective	*river*	noun
bridge	noun	*splash*	interjection

You may have noticed that I omitted the word 'the' (see TIP 2).

TIP 2 Article
The article ('the', 'a', 'an') may be definite or indefinite.
An article indicates that the next word will be a noun. A noun may have one or more preceding adjectives, as in the last three examples below: *a walk; an elephant; an effort; the filing cabinet; the enormous black clouds; the shiny, new, black leather belt*

TIP 3 Article: definite
The definite article is the word 'the'.
This is placed in front of a noun and is used to enable the noun to refer to something already known to both the speaker/writer and the listener/reader:
The bedspread is made from antique silk. The raspberries are not yet ready to eat.

TIP 4 Article: indefinite
The indefinite article doesn't specify any particular noun. Use 'a' before a consonant (*a bicycle*) and 'an' before a vowel (*an apple*):
A cat is smaller than an elephant.

TIP 5 Noun: common
A common noun is the name of a person, place or thing, often preceded by a definite or indefinite article: *girl, pencil, cupboard*

TIP 6 Noun: proper
A proper noun has a capital letter and refers to a particular person, place or thing:
Albert Einstein, New York, The Mona Lisa

TIP 7 Noun: abstract
An abstract noun describes abstract feelings, states and qualities. These nouns can't be touched. Often, there is no definite or indefinite article: *height, happiness, age*

Let's try this with and without an article: *Happiness is something we all strive for.*
The happiness shown on her face was a delight to see.

TIP 8 Noun: collective
A collective noun indicates a group of some kind: *jury, class, audience*

The verb used with a collective noun can vary; but a collective noun is normally followed by a singular verb: *The government is changing its policy on university funding. The government are changing their policy on university funding.*

In British English (BrE), it's often acceptable to use either a singular or a plural verb after a collective noun. American English (AmE) prefers a singular verb. Here, I'm in agreement with AmE, as in the first example above.

If in doubt, work out whether the collective noun is thought of as a unit, or whether the members of this unit are considered as individuals or single items: *The team was not united. The team were not united.*

If you wish, you can insert a word such as 'members' and make the verb very definitely plural: *The members of the team were not united.*

Note

Of course, some collective nouns do have a plural, so they would then require plural verbs:
Ten choirs were singing in the competition.
The classes all begin next week.

TIP 9 Noun: countable
To differentiate the two different classes of nouns, they are sometimes referred to as countable and uncountable (or count and uncount) nouns.

Countable nouns refer to items you can count, however large the number:
day, horse, cup

Countable nouns may be singular or plural: *day/days, horse/horses, cup/cups*

Singular countable nouns need a determiner (TIP 47): *this day, the horse, my cup, a race*

Plural countable nouns can be used without a determiner: *Days are… Horses run… Cups break… Races take place…*

TIP 10 Noun: uncountable
advice, currency, furniture, information, luggage, money, music, news, power, rice, sand, travel, work

Uncountable nouns require a singular verb:
The information is on your seat. Travel gives pleasure to all. Bad news spreads quickly.

Uncountable nouns don't normally require an indefinite article:
Work of one kind or another occupies us all. He gave me good advice.

'Some', 'any', 'little' and 'much' can be used with uncountable nouns:
some help, any rice, little furniture, much power

TIP 11 Noun: countable and uncountable
Some nouns may be both countable and uncountable:
Many people drink wine. The wines of California… We all need water. People drink the waters at many spas. Power is desired by some. She has supernatural powers.

 Drinks are usually uncountable. However, since drinks come in a container, you can say: *two teas, six coffees*

TIP 12 Noun: suffixes
A suffix (word ending) can indicate a noun:

–tion	*examination*	*action*
–ness	*kindness*	*idleness*
–ity	*charity*	*infinity*
–hood	*childhood*	*livelihood*
–ment	*statement*	*comment*

Which of the four types of noun (common, proper, abstract, collective) are these?

TIP 13 Noun: gerund (Advanced Point)
Verbal nouns or gerunds look like the present participle (TIP 42):
Losing is disappointing. Walking is good for you.

Look at two more incorrect examples: *There was no hope of the climber reaching the top that day.* ✗ *She understood him being angry.* ✗

Now, the correct versions: *There was no hope of the climber's reaching the top that day.* ✓ *She understood his being angry.* ✓

You need the possessive here. However, most people would say: *There was no hope of the climber reaching the top that day*, something which may become acceptable through usage.

What's wrong with this? Gerunds can cause mistakes, where an object pronoun (TIP 68), 'him', is used instead of a possessive adjective, 'his' (TIP 54). If you want to know more about gerunds (and gerundives, which are not covered here) look in a comprehensive grammar book.

Note

Let's look at a related point, sometimes called the 'dangling or misrelated participle or modifier'. Misused, these can cause amusement, as in the first example below. One example below is used correctly, the other two not. See whether you can decide which is which and why:
Driving along the road, a dog ran towards the car.
Walking up the hill, I quickly became tired.
As a valued customer, I should like to tell you about our new product.

You probably chose the first and third as incorrect. Why are they wrong?

It's because the person/animal in the first part of the sentence is not the same as the one after the comma. In the second, they are the same. So, that's what you need to consider if you write a similar sentence, and rewrite accordingly.

To correct the first and third one above, write: *While I was driving along the road, a dog ran towards the car. As a valued customer, you will be interested in our new product.*

This error is quite common, and it's grammatical nonsense when it does appear.

TIP 14 Verb: what is it?
A verb states what someone or something is doing or is. Verbs refer to both actions and situations/states.

Action or doing verbs: *read, work, sleep*

State verbs convey the idea of occurrence or existence:
appear, be, belong to, contain, exist, feel, like, need, see, seem, sound, surprise

The latter are rarely used on their own. You may be able to think of times when you can use them alone (*it appeared*), but normally they need a complement (TIP 36) or an object (TIP 32) to complete the sense.

One of the factors which has made English into the world language it is today is that few nouns change their word endings (unlike, for example, German). However, the verb does change. Here is an example:

The verb 'to take' has five forms: *take, takes, took, taken, taking*

TIP 15 Verb: tense

Present tense	Past tense	Future tense
I am	*I was*	*I shall be*
You take	*You took*	*You will take*
He runs	*He ran*	*He will run*

A verb may be just one word, 'begin', but it often has more than one part to it. This changes, depending on whether the verb is in the present, the past or the future tense: *The party begins/is beginning/does begin. The party began/was beginning/did begin. The party will begin/will be beginning, etc.*

If I use different names for tenses and other grammatical terms from those you are familiar with, just replace these with whatever you are used to.

TIP 16 Verb: future
English has no formal future tense (unlike e.g. French or Latin, where the verb ending shows future meaning).

Here are the three ways in English of expressing the future: **shall or will** (TIP 23), **going to, future-time adverbs** (e.g. tomorrow) **with the present tense:** *I shall see you on Thursday. We're going to take our books back to the library. Amanda plays in a concert in Bath next week.*

TIP 17 Verb: regular and irregular
The regular verb past tense ending is –ed: *walked, visited, touched*

Irregular verbs have different endings in the past tense and the past participle form.

Look at the past participles over the page. You need the verb 'to have' in order to form the past tense.

Present	Past	Past participle

1. Verbs which don't change:

hit	*hit*	*(I have) hit*
let	*let*	*(she has) let*
shut	*shut*	*(you have) shut*

2. Verbs with one change:

hear	*heard*	*heard*
make	*made*	*made*
sell	*sold*	*sold*

3. Verbs with two changes:

eat	*ate*	*eaten*
see	*saw*	*seen*
take	*took*	*taken*

If English is your second language, you'll have learned these. For those of you whose first language is English, these will come naturally.

 Pay particular attention to the simple past tense of the following two verbs, where the one-letter difference is not always noticed: *She bought (buy) two suitcases. She brought (bring) two suitcases.*

A good dictionary gives the past tenses of verbs. If none is given, the verb is regular, so just add –ed to the infinitive (TIP 38).

TIP 18 Verb: main
A simple sentence has one main verb: *She swims in the lake. Please write the letter today. Have you finished your work?*

TIP 19 Verb: auxiliary
The main auxiliary (or helping) verbs are 'to be', 'to have' and 'to do'.

TIP 20 Verb: auxiliary verbs to form tenses
These auxiliary verbs help to form past and future tenses by adding to other verbs:
I shall cut, I have made, you will have forgotten, do watch out!

TIP 21 Verb: modal auxiliaries (Advanced Point)
The modal auxiliary verbs are:
can, could, may, might, must, ought, shall, should, will, would

They have no infinitives. Instead, use 'to be able to', 'to be allowed to', 'to have to', etc.:
He used to have to get up at 6 o'clock. She hoped to be allowed to catch the early train.

Modal verbs are used with other verbs and in question tags (TIP 22).

> **Note**
>
> **Phrasal verbs are verbs with an added preposition or other word.** This enables the 'bare' verb (TIP 38) to take on a large number of meanings. Phrasal verbs can strike terror into the hearts of those learning English as a Second Language but, if you're a native speaker, you'll be familiar with the differences the second words make to such verbs as these:
>
> *Take: action/after/apart/away/down/in/off/out/over/time/to/up*
> *Break: away/down/in/into/off/out/up/cover*

Think of at least three prepositions which could follow 'bring' and 'put'. If *you* can't, your dictionary can.

TIP 22 Verb: question tags
A question tag is a structure in which a statement or a command is turned into a question by adding an interrogative (question) fragment (the 'tag').

These are very straightforward, and you'll have used them many times, even if you didn't know the grammatical term:
You mustn't do that, must you? He could do that, couldn't he?

Note how, when the first statement is negative, the question tag is positive – and vice versa. Try making some more question tags with other modal verbs from TIP 21.

Note also that there is a comma before the question tag.

TIP 23 Verb: shall and will
The main use of 'shall' and 'will' is to form the future tense. In Standard English, 'shall' is used for the first person (I, we, TIP 37), and 'will' for the others (you, he/she/it, they): *I shall begin, you (singular) will begin, he/she/it/one will begin, we shall begin, you (plural) will begin, they will begin*

However, in the first person, you'll normally hear and say *I'll begin* or *we'll begin*.

TIP 24 Verb: other uses of shall
'Shall' can express command, obligation, necessity or permission. However, this is rarely used: *You shall not do that! We shall overcome.*

Grammar books often state that the future is expressed as in TIP 23 above; and to express command, obligation, necessity or permission, just reverse the rule (i.e. 'will' with the first person and 'shall' with all the rest). That's fine. But don't worry too much about this distinction – just say what feels best for you! .

TIP 25 Verb: other uses of will
'Will' (including the first person) can be used to express determination, intention, willingness and wish: *I will see her, whatever he thinks.*

Will can also express a command: *You* will *shut the door!*

TIP 26 Verb: should, would, ought

'Should' is a tense of 'shall', expressing obligation. 'Ought (to)' has the same meaning: *I should have worked harder. I ought to have worked harder.*

'Would' is a tense of 'will' in its sense of determination, intention, willingness, wish: *He wouldn't hurry.* (He had no intention of hurrying.) **This is called the conditional tense:** *I should be delighted if you would help. We should like to ask your son to come. It would be helpful if you could come too.*

Many people use 'would' for the first two examples above.

TIP 27 Verb: can or may

In formal English statements, there is a clear distinction between 'can' and 'may'.

1. 'Can' refers to the ability to do something:

I can swim. (I am able to swim.) *He can count to ten.*

2. 'May' refers to permission or probability:

May I leave now? (Am I allowed to leave now?) *He may fall asleep.*

Informally, many people would say: *Can I leave now?*

TIP 28 Verb: can, may; might, could

'May' has links with 'can', and 'might' with 'could'.

Let's see them incorrectly first: *If he could run faster, he may win the race.* ✗
If he can run faster, he might win the race. ✗
To put these right: *If he can run faster, he may win the race.* ✓
If he could run faster, he might win the race. ✓

Get your ear attuned to this one.

TIP 29 Verb: subject

The subject of the verb is the person or thing that does or is that verb.

How do you find the subject of a sentence? Ask yourself who or what is doing or being the verb. Let's look at this: *Stephen cut my hair.*

Who cut my hair? Stephen, of course, so 'Stephen' is the subject, and 'cut' (past tense) is the verb. Stephen is a proper noun. Let's try with a common noun and a pronoun: *The stylist cut my hair. He cut my hair.*

I'm sure you can find the subjects.

TIP 30 Verb: finite
A verb with a tense and a subject is called a finite verb.

Learn the terms 'tense', 'subject' and 'finite verb', as they will recur. Before you continue, check that you understand and will remember these terms by finding five fairly short sentences elsewhere in this book or any other document you have around and picking out their subjects and verbs (plus the tense of the verb).

 You may like to observe how, in usage, nouns are turning into verbs. For a long time, we've had examples that are firmly part of the language: 'ring', 'sleep', 'drive', 'draw', which can be both nouns and verbs. Then there were 'carpet', 'hospitalise', etc., which are now acceptable. Listen for new examples of this trend. Here are two: *The player was stretchered off the field and later helicoptered to hospital.*

This is just one example of how language is constantly changing.

A trend you should try to resist is to answer a question with the 'wrong' verb, as here:
Q. *Have you got a pen?*
A. *Yes, I do.*

I would reply: *Yes, I have.*

However, this change of verb is so common now in some countries, particularly the United States and Australia, that it's becoming the norm.

 TIP 31
Verb: agreement with subject
Sometimes called concord, this is the way in which a particular form of one word (the subject) requires the use of the corresponding form of another word (the verb). In other words, the verb must agree with its subject.

To find the subject of a verb, ask yourself who or what is doing the action of the verb or is the state of the verb.

Let's return to the most important verb – 'to be'. You'll remember the present tense:
I am, you are (just one you, a singular you), *he/she/it/one is, we are, you are* (more than one you, a plural you), *they are*

And the past tense: *I was, you were* (just one you, a singular you), *he/she/it/one was, we were, you were* (more than one you, a plural you), *they were*

With a noun rather than a pronoun as the subject, the same rules as for 'he/she/it/they' are followed, depending on whether the noun is singular or plural: *The boy (he) is ... The man and the woman (they) are ...*

Look at the next examples. Which are correct? If you choose any as correct, can you explain why?
1. *A new set of proposals have been considered.*
2. *The writer's unfamiliarity with verbs are hindering his career.*
3. *The chance of making mistakes with these are greater if you don't understand subject and verb.*
4. *An ability to show common sense and initiative is required of all candidates.*
5. *We'll have to see what the basis of these allegations are.*
6. *Insurance and a passport is needed.*

Is any sentence correct? Yes, one.

These are the subjects (with the verb corrected):
1. *set (has)*
2. *The writer's unfamiliarity (is)*
3. *chance (is)*
4. *An ability is (correct)*
5. *basis (is)*
6. *Insurance and a passport (are)*

The first type of error occurs when the subject and verb are a long way from each other and a plural word (incorrectly given preference) is next to the verb, as in 1, 2, 3 and 5. The larger number of examples reflects that this is the more common way that this error is made.

It's often called the mistake of the nearest noun. What happens is that the writer, being unaware that the subject and verb must agree, sees a plural word just before s/he wants to write or say a verb and assumes that the verb must be plural.

So, remember that you may have to look further back in the sentence to find your subject (and the correct verb). When I wrote the six sentences above, my spellchecker stopped me with the message: 'Subject-Verb Agreement' in all cases except 4.

The second type of error is where two subjects are joined together as if they were one thing and given a singular verb (see 6 above).

Joining two words with 'and' and treating them as one singular compound subject is fine provided that the two items are normally together and considered to be one idea: *Fish and chips is not my favourite meal.* ✓
'Pride and Prejudice' is a novel by Jane Austen. ✓

Spend some time finding subjects and verbs until you're certain that you'll always know what and where these are in the future. You may need to work at this point before it becomes automatic and you pick up incorrect usage of this whenever it occurs. Listen to the television or read newspapers critically; you'll soon come across some errors. Finding them yourself is the best way for you to learn how not to make mistakes in this vital point.

TIP 32 Verb: object
A basic sentence looks like this:

Subject	Verb	Object
She	*eats*	*cheese.*
The cat	*chased*	*the mouse.*

An object is the person or thing to whom or what the action of the verb is done (*cheese, the mouse*).

TIP 33 Verb: transitive
Any verb that can take an object is known as a transitive verb. This is because the action of the verb is transferred or carried over to the object.

Both verbs in TIP 32 are transitive. Now, two more examples: *She touched her toes, and then put on her socks and shoes. He washed his hands, and then ate the sandwich.*

Test by checking if they answer the question 'what' immediately after the verb, e.g. 'She touched what?'

How many objects? Five: 'toes', 'socks', 'shoes', 'hands' and 'sandwich', all answering the question 'what' of their respective verbs.

Now, find some more objects in other sentences.

Did you notice the phrasal verb in the first example?

TIP 34 Verb: intransitive
A verb which doesn't take an object is known as an intransitive verb:
The sun set below the horizon. They came to my house.

Try the 'what' test immediately after the verb. It doesn't work. In the first, it does answer the question 'where', but that doesn't make 'below the horizon' an object. It's a prepositional phrase, which you'll be introduced to later (TIP 78).

TIP 35 Verb: transitive and intransitive (Advanced Point)
Some verbs may be both transitive and intransitive (a good dictionary will give examples): *Think of something to say. She thought sad thoughts. He flew to Boston. He flew a passenger plane.*

Work out which are transitive and which are intransitive with the 'what' test. Remember to ask 'what' immediately after the verb.

TIP 36 Verb: linking or complement (Advanced Point)
Some verbs are always intransitive because they never take an object. **Other verbs, however, take a complement to complete the sense. These are called linking verbs:** *to be, to seem, to appear, to become, to feel, to smell, to taste, to sound*

The bread tasted good! The proposal seemed ideal. She appeared intelligent. He became a professor.

If you stop after the verb in the examples above, you'll see that they are incomplete without the next word (three adjectives and one noun).

Although these answer the question 'what' after the verb, remember that, with these verbs, the word coming after the verb is a complement and *not* an object.

TIP 37 Verb: person
Look again at the verb 'to be': *I am, you are, he/she/it/one is, we are, you are, they are*

Now, look at the words before the verb (here pronouns, TIP 69).

You've probably heard the terms 'the first person', 'the second person', etc.

Here are the personal subject and object pronouns:
First person: *I, we* (subject)   *me, us* (object)
Second person: *you* (subject)   *you* (object)
Third person: *he, she, it, one, they* (subject)   *him, her, it, one, them* (object)

I like you (subject, verb, object).
You like me (subject, verb, object).

Most novels are written in the third person, i.e. writing as if the story happened to someone else. If you find a book written in the first person, this may be an autobiography or, if it's a novel, the book is written as if the main character is speaking to you. You may find a book written in the second person, but this is much less usual. In the case of a novel, it's as if the action is happening to 'you', the reader.

When you read novels, work out which person they're written in. Also, look at other pieces of writing you have around: emails, letters, reports, newspaper articles. Which person are they written in? Which person is this book written in?

TIP 38 Verb: infinitive
As you know, a finite verb has a subject.

1. An infinitive (an *infinite* verb) does not. Infinitives are introduced by 'to':
to break, to win, to grow, to stand, to go

"To err is human; to forgive, divine." [Alexander Pope]

How many infinitives are there in the last example above?

The infinitive without 'to' is known as the bare infinitive. Whenever you look a verb up in a dictionary, you'll find it in the bare infinitive form, without 'to'.

2. The infinitive has both active and passive forms (TIP 40):

Active	**Passive**
to choose	*to be chosen*
to wear	*to be worn*

3. Infinitives can be in the present tense: *to break, to win, to grow, to stand, to go*

4. Or the past tense: *to have broken, to have won, to have grown, to have stood, to have gone*

5. Or the continuous tenses: *to be breaking, to be winning, to be growing, to have been standing, to have been going*

6. There is no future infinitive, so this has to be shown by using 'to be about to':
We were about to leave when it started to rain heavily.

TIP 39 Verb: infinitive – to split or to not split
Let's look now at the somewhat contentious issue of splitting the infinitive, something which more people complain about than can say what is grammatically 'wrong' with it (see also TIP 302).

To explain: in order to split an infinitive, an adverb must be inserted between 'to' and the verb. One of the most quoted examples of this you may know: *"to boldly go…"* [Star Trek]

With the words in this order, this is far more memorable than would be *to go boldly.*

And another split infinitive (the second one in this sentence):
"To err is human, but to really foul things up requires a computer."

In many other languages (including French, e.g. *manger* 'to eat'), it's impossible to split the infinitive, as it consists of only one word. So 'experts' say you should never do this.

What do I think? I don't particularly like it, but there's nothing intrinsically wrong, so even I do this on occasions. Your choice!

Scientists are trying to finally wipe out tuberculosis. I wanted to really get it right this time. To split or to not split.

Let's give the last word to the novelist Raymond Chandler: *"Would you convey my compliments to the purist who reads your proofs and tell him or her that… when I split an infinitive, I split it so it will stay split."*

TIP 40 Verb: active and passive voice

1. A verb is in the active voice when the subject of the verb is performing the action of the verb: *The child ate the apple.*
"God made the country, and man made the town." [William Cowper]

2. In the passive voice, the subject of the verb has the action of the verb done to him/her/it/them: *The apple was eaten by the child.*
The birthday cake was made by the child's grandmother.

Note how passive sentences often contain 'by' someone.

The passive is often used when what happens is more important than the person or thing that does or did it: *A ring had been stolen. Dinner will be served at eight.*

It's accepted that the use of the active and the avoidance of the passive produces a good strong style.

TIP 41 Verb: mood (Advanced Point)

The verb has three moods/modes: **indicative, imperative, subjunctive.**

A verb in the indicative mood states a fact: *The cat sat on his lap throughout the meeting.*

Or asks a question: *What time is it?*

The imperative gives a command: *Don't do that!*

The subjunctive is used far less often – and far less accurately, except by a few. Advance warning of a subjunctive may be marked by the appearance of 'if', 'that' or, very infrequently, 'lest' (see examples below).

It's likely that you won't even be aware that you're using the subjunctive, as the form of the verb is often the same as the indicative (except in the verb 'to be').

It may be used to indicate a condition, a purpose, or a wish: *I wish that I were tall!*
He insisted that she return (not 'returns') *the ring. "If we should fail…"* [William Shakespeare] *"Lest we forget…"* (The opportunity to use 'lest' doesn't arise very often!)

You'll hear: *"I wish that I was wealthy."* Fine in informal speech.

As you see from the first example above, the subjunctive of the verb 'to be' looks very different from the indicative:

Indicative	Subjunctive
I am	*I be, were*
you are	*you be, were*
he/she is	*he/she be, were*
we are	*we be, were*
they are	*they be, were*

He insisted that he be given permission to go at once. They requested that they be given better seats. Would that it were all true. I wish (that) you were not so quick.

In this last example, even if you omit 'that', this word is still understood to be there. 'Were' looks like the past tense of 'is', but is in fact the past subjunctive, which can refer to the present or the future. Phew!

Let's see some examples with 'if', beginning with arguably the most commonly used: *If I were you…* (The incorrect *If I was you…* is heard all the time.) *He spoke to her as if she were a fool. What if she were to come later?*

Now for a few expressions in the subjunctive with which you'll be familiar: *Far be it from me… Be that as it may… Come what may. If need be. So be it.*

Let's end this by considering the following, written in 1941: *"The subjunctive mood is in its death throes, and the best thing to do is to put it out of its misery as soon as possible."* [Somerset Maugham]

TIP 42 Verb: present participle
Present participles are formed from the infinitive, plus –ing. Sometimes, you may need to double the final consonant, as in 'putting', 'stopping', etc: *walking, creeping, seeing*

These are needed to form the present continuous tense: *They are walking along the beach. "Yes, madam, Nature is creeping up."* [James McNeill Whistler] *I'm seeing her next week.*

TIP 43 Verb: past participle
The past participle (the part of the verb which follows 'have') ends in –d, –ed, –t, etc.: *found, pointed, taught*

Let's first see how verbs change – or don't change – in the present and past:

Present	Simple past	Present perfect

Some verbs use the same word throughout:

cut	*cut*	*have cut*
upset	*upset*	*have upset*

Others have one change:

feel	*felt*	*have felt*
pay	*paid*	*have paid*

Or two changes:

go	*went*	*have gone*
give	*gave*	*have given*

So, the past participle is the third one, the word after 'have'.

TIP 44 Verb: direct and indirect speech
Speech can be either direct or indirect/reported.

1. **Direct speech requires inverted commas:** *"My idea of an agreeable person," said Hugo Bohun, "is a person who agrees with me."* [Benjamin Disraeli]
"I never wear brown in London." [Lord Curzon]

2. **Indirect speech is the reporting of something spoken or written:**
Lord Curzon stated/said (that) he never wore brown in London.

Look at the changes:
* A verb of saying is used
* No inverted commas
* 'I' becomes 'he'
* 'Wear' becomes 'wore': past tense instead of present
* An optional 'that' is inserted

Try putting some direct speech, either spoken or from a book, into indirect speech.

TIP 45 Verb: either... or, neither... nor
Both of these require singular verbs: *Either Bob Hope or Phil Silvers was America's favourite comedian. Neither Ruby Wax nor Joan Rivers makes her laugh.*

Use 'either... or' with positive statements and 'neither... nor' with negative statements.

But don't mix up the two, as in this incorrect example:
Neither Mary or Margaret looked at each other in the library. ✘

I'm sure you don't say something like this: *I don't like rhubarb. Me neither.* ✘

This should be 'neither do I' or 'nor do I', as there is a negative in the first sentence.

Remember the comment at the end of TIP 30? This is a similar error:
You've either got it or you don't. ✗

Can you put this right before looking at the answer below?
You've either got it or you haven't. ✓

TIP 46 Verb: each, none, nothing

1. **Each**

When each is the subject of a verb, it must have a singular verb:
Each of them was eager to go first. This means 'each one of'.

If you continue as in this example, use a singular pronoun:
Each of them was doing his/her (not their) shopping.

2. **None**

None may take a singular or a plural verb. I usually use a singular verb, because, after all, you can't get more singular than less than one! You have to decide each case on its merits. Look at these: *None of the money was recovered.* ✓
None of them were/was able to come. ✓

3. **Nothing**

Nothing always takes a singular verb: *Nothing of the vast piles of food was left.*
Nothing except pleasure, joy and happiness is to be found on the island.

TIP 47 Adjective: determiner

The adjective's main role is to be used with a noun to express (for example) quantity, number and possession. The following words are used to qualify nouns and are called determiners:
1. Articles (*a, an, the*)
2. Numbers (*one, two, three…*)
3. Quantifiers (*some, any, few, many, no, each, every, such, another…*)
4. Demonstrative adjectives (*this, that, these, those*)
5. Possessive adjectives (*my, your, her, our…*)
a computer, an effort, the dog, ten letters, few women, this evening, these people, those days, that pen, my umbrella, your house

There can be other adjectives after the determiner and in front of the noun: *a new computer, an enormous effort, the friendly dog, ten unopened letters, few young women, this beautiful evening, those perfect days, that new pen, my green umbrella, these friendly people, your new house*

TIP 48 Adjective: position

An adjective answers the questions 'how many?', 'what kind of?', etc.

1. The normal place for an adjective in English is in front of the noun it describes or qualifies: *a thin girl, the last day, good news*

Read something around you and find some adjectives. Where are most of them?

2. You may find they come after a verb. Do you remember linking verbs (TIP 36)? **These verbs include 'to be', 'to become', 'to seem', 'to appear', 'to taste', 'to smell', 'to sound'.** Such verbs are incomplete without a noun or an adjective to complete the sense, so let's look at some with adjectives:
The food tasted wonderful. The girl appeared confident. He looked younger.

> **Note** Sometimes an adjective can work as a noun:
> *the hungry, the young, the poor*

TIP 49 Adjective: order
There are rules on order when there is more than one adjective in front of a noun:
He was chasing a lovely brown (not a 'brown lovely') *Tamworth pig.*

Why this order? **Because *opinion* is followed by *fact*.** The opinion is that it's lovely; the fact is that it's brown.

If there are several adjectives of fact, you must normally put them in this order:
size, age, shape, colour, origin, material

So, to return to the pig: *He was chasing a large, old, brown Tamworth pig.*

Of course, these are far more adjectives than one would use – though sometimes you might use three or even four. Style dictates that adjectives should be used sparingly.

To return to the opinion adjective: if you were to use one here, it would have to precede all the others: *He was chasing a lovely, large, old, brown Tamworth pig.*

See whether you can describe one object with three or four adjectives in the correct order.

TIP 50 Adjective: list separated by commas
When there is a long list of adjectives in front of a noun, they are normally separated by commas: *He was chasing a lovely, large, old, brown Tamworth pig.*

Have a look at the last two adjectives, 'Tamworth pig'. When adjectives (particularly the last one) are in a close relationship to the noun, the commas are omitted:
that awful old coat, my new blue skirt

TIP 51 Adjective: degrees of comparison

When two or more people or things are compared, the form of the adjective changes. Learn these terms: positive, comparative, superlative, known as the degrees of comparison.

1. One-syllable adjectives. When you compare two things, add –er to the positive form; and when you compare three or more things, add –est:

Positive	Comparative	Superlative
fat	*fatter*	*fattest*
slow	*slower*	*slowest*

2. –er and –est may also be added to two-syllable adjectives, unless the new word sounds awkward:
happy, happier, happiest   *healthy, healthier, healthiest*

If a two-syllable adjective sounds awkward, use 'more' and 'most':
more handsome   *most handsome*

3. For all three-syllable adjectives, use 'more' or 'most':
more interesting   *most interesting*
more mysterious   *most mysterious*

4. These are examples of where you can use either:
cleverer   *more clever*
narrower   *more narrow*
quieter   *more quiet*
simpler   *more simple*

5. And in the superlative:
the cleverest   *the most clever*
the narrowest   *the most narrow*
the quietest   *the most quiet*
the simplest   *the most simple*

6. Use the comparative when comparing two things: *Andrew is taller than Ben is.*
N.B. The word 'than' is frequently used in comparisons.

7. Use the superlative when comparing three or more things:
Roger is taller than Sophie is, but Douglas is the tallest.

The word 'the' is frequently used in superlatives:
Mt Everest is the highest mountain in the world.

8. A common mistake is to use the superlative instead of the comparative:
Which of you is the youngest – you or your brother? ✗
Which of you is the younger – you or your brother? ✓

 **TIP 52**
Adjective: common exceptions
Some very common adjectives are irregular, so have to be learned:

Positive	Comparative	Superlative
bad	*worse*	*worst*
far (distance)	*farther*	*farthest*
far (extent)	*further*	*furthest*
good	*better*	*best*
ill	*worse*	*worst*
late	*later*	*latest* or *last*
little	*less*	*least*
little (size)	*littler*	*littlest*
many	*more*	*most*
much	*more*	*most*

Let's look at two examples: *"Discretion is not the better part of biography."* [Lytton Strachey] *"It was the best of times, it was the worst of times…"* [Charles Dickens]

TIP 53 Adjective: demonstrative
This, that, these, those
These are not difficult, but are used incorrectly sometimes by those who don't think:
I do hate those kinds of people. ✖ *These sorts of games are boring.* ✖

Put them in the singular: *I do hate this kind of person.* ✔ *This sort of game is boring.* ✔

TIP 54 Adjective: possessive
These adjectives show possession or ownership: *my, your, his, her, its, our, their, whose*

Your birthday is on the same day as my mother's. His car was stolen from the garage.

TIP 55 Adjective: each and every
'Each' and 'every' have similar but not always the same meanings.

1. **Let's look first at when they mean the same:** *Prices go up each year. Prices go up every year.*

2. **When the meanings are different, use a singular verb with 'each' and 'every':**
Each boy takes his turn (one by one). *Every boy takes his turn* (all).

3. **You can use 'of' with 'each', but not with 'every':** *Each of the boys takes his turn.*

4. **For two things, use 'each', but not 'every':** *He had a bag in each hand.*

5. **For more than two things, say 'every':** *For every person who studies this course, there may be 20 who don't make the effort to complete it.*
The boat leaves every 20 minutes.

TIP 56 Adjective: more and most
Use more to compare two things: *We have more post in the week than at the weekend.*
Use most to compare three or more things: *We have most letters at Christmas.*

TIP 57 Adjective: some and any
1. **Some** means 'an unspecified number or amount' and is only used with positive statements: *some cheese; some grass; some friends;*
"Please, sir, I want some more." [Charles Dickens]

Some is used in a question where the answer 'yes' is expected: *May I have some butter?*

2. **Any** means 'one of several' and is sometimes used with negative statements and questions: *"Baa, baa, black sheep, have you any wool?"*
Haven't you got any money?

TIP 58 Adjective: suffixes
Some **suffixes** are characteristic of adjectives:
–able	*manageable*
–ible	*credible*
–ous	*infamous*

TIP 59 Adjective: pitfalls with comparisons
Let's look at two pitfalls that can happen when comparing adjectives:

1. **Make sure to compare like with like:** *The citizens of New York are wealthier than Mumbai.* ✗ (Put this way, it appears as if a population is being compared with a city.)
Make sure you balance the comparison to make it clear: *The citizens of New York are wealthier than those of Mumbai.* ✓

2. **Take care not to use a double comparison:** *The results arrived more quicker than I had expected.* ✗ *The boy was more angrier than I had feared he would be.* ✗
The first one should be: *The results arrived more quickly than I had expected.* ✓

Try the second one, which can be done in two ways.

TIP 60 Adverb: how, when, where
An adverb adds to or 'modifies' a verb and tells you how, when or where the action of the verb happened.

An adverb is often an adjective plus 'ly': *slowly, beautifully*

So, let's add these to a verb: *The van drove slowly. She sang beautifully.*
The adverbs above tell you how the subjects (the van, she) drove and sang.

Now, let's look at when or where something happened:
It happened today. It happened there.

Put the adverb as close as you can to the verb it is modifying: *He played well despite his injury. She spoke quietly to her friend.*

TIP 61 Adverb: degrees of comparison

Like adjectives, adverbs have degrees of comparison. You normally have to add 'more' and 'most' to the adverb:

slowly	*more slowly*	*most slowly*
beautifully	*more beautifully*	*most beautifully*
quietly	*more quietly*	*most quietly*

It's not considered good style to use 'quicker' as an adverb. Use 'more quickly' and use 'quicker' for the comparative form of the adjective only: *I work more quickly* (adverb) *in the mornings. I work at a quicker* (adjective) *speed in the mornings.*

TIP 62
Adverb: common exceptions

Here's a list of common exceptions when comparing adverbs:

Positive	Comparative	Superlative
badly	*worse*	*worst*
far (extent)	*further*	*furthest*
ill	*worse*	*worst*
late	*later*	*latest* or *last*
little (amount)	*less*	*least*
much	*more*	*most*
well	*better*	*best*

TIP 63 Adverb: conjunctive

Conjunctive adverbs join parts of a sentence. The list includes:
also, besides, furthermore, however, indeed, instead, moreover, next, anyway, nevertheless, otherwise, so, therefore, thus

When you use one of these at the beginning of a sentence, you must put a comma after it: *Anyway, there were only three left. Moreover, Angela had forgotten the knives.*

Try a few more yourself.

TIP 64 Adverb: modifying an adjective

An adverb sometimes modifies an adjective: *The woman was very old.* 'Very' is an adverb modifying 'old', which is an adjective describing the noun 'woman'.

Adverbs don't always end in 'ly'. Here are some which don't: *always, before, even, fast, here, last, quite, sometimes, soon, still, then, today, tomorrow, too, very, yesterday*

You may be thinking that some of these words are adjectives. You could be right – in context: *The fast driver…* (adjective) ✔ *The man drove fast* (adverb). ✔

Find another which could be both an adjective and an adverb.

Always ask yourself what work a word is doing in the sentence – and/or look it up in your dictionary.

Note | Some words which end in 'ly' are not adverbs, so don't assume that every word ending in 'ly' is automatically an adverb: *ugly, friendly, lonely* (all adjectives)

TIP 65 Adverb: modifying another adverb

The third part of speech an adverb can modify is another adverb: *He ran very quickly. She sang rather quietly.*

TIP 66
Adverb: use of adjective for adverb

I'm not sure what it is about adverbs that makes people reluctant to use them, preferring to use incorrect adjectives instead. Laziness? Ignorance? Possibly the latter.

Remember that an adverb adds to a verb, so don't write or say: *He ran magnificent.* ✘ *She spoke brilliant.* ✘

What's wrong here? 'Magnificent' and 'brilliant' are adjectives, so must qualify nouns.

Remember, an adjective adds to a noun; and an adverb adds to a verb.

Whereas, in most cases, both adjective and adverb are very similar in spelling, there are exceptions, e.g. 'good' and 'well'. A kind of mental blockage can occur here: *The golfer was good.* ✔ *The golfer played good.* ✘

In the first example, 'good' (adjective) is correctly describing the noun 'golfer'. In the second, it's incorrectly modifying the verb 'played'. What is needed is the adverb 'well'.

This is a very common mistake. **Learn that adverbs must not be confused with adjectives.**

TIP 67 Pronoun

A pronoun is a word used instead of a noun. It's poor style to keep repeating a noun, so use a pronoun. This is how to do it: *The boy ran across the road. The boy was seven.*

It doesn't take a genius to improve this: *The boy ran across the road. He was seven.*

Best, of course, would be: *The seven-year-old boy ran across the road.*

TIP 68 Pronoun: subject and object

1. **Subject pronouns:** *I, you, he, she, it, we, they, who*
He cleaned the windows.

2. **Object pronouns:** *me, you, him, her, it, us, them, whom*
The man saw him.

3. **Pronouns with compound subjects and objects:** A sentence such as the following is wrong: *Anita and me went to the theatre.* ✘

To test, just try the sentences like this: *Anita went to the theatre.* ✔ *Me went to the theatre.* ✘ *I went to the theatre.* ✔

So the correct version must be: *Anita and I went to the theatre.* ✔

'I' is a subject pronoun and 'me' is an object pronoun. Subject pronouns are needed here, as the subject of the verb 'went'.

Similarly, these are also wrong: *He likes Judy and I.* ✘ *My uncle left the property to my sister and I.* ✘ *My uncle left the property to her and I.* ✘

Let's look at the first one: *She likes Judy.* ✔ *She likes I.* ✘ *She likes me.* ✔

So you get: *She likes Judy and me.* ✔

Now, you try the others.

Incidentally, it's correct (and polite) to put 'I', 'we', 'me' or 'us' (the first person) last – but some people don't seem to be aware of that!
She likes me, my sister and Judy. ✘
She likes Judy, my sister and me. ✔

TIP 69 Pronoun: reflexive
Reflexive pronouns must obey the rule of concord (TIP 31) and agree with the subject. Although reflexive verbs are common in some languages, e.g. French and Italian, English uses them less frequently. But here are two:
I washed myself. They washed themselves.

Don't say: *Bill and myself went to the cinema.* ✘
But: *Bill and I went to the cinema.* ✔

I once saw: *'the most notable being when myself and Emma took over...'* ✘
'Myself' cannot be substituted for 'I'. It can only be used *in addition to* 'I'. Similarly with 'themselves' and all the other reflexive pronouns. Note how the writer has put himself before the other person, too!

TIP 70 Pronoun: verbs with complements (Advanced Point)
A pronoun that follows a linking verb is a *subject* pronoun (TIP 68).

The correct usage below may sound pedantic, but you may need it on occasions:
It is I. ✓ (Though most people, of course, say 'It's me'.)
It was he (not 'him') *who came first.* ✓

TIP 71 Pronoun: possessive
These pronouns show ownership: *mine, yours, his, hers, ours, theirs, whose*
That house is theirs. Whose is that box?

TIP 72 Pronoun: interrogative
This is the pronoun that asks a question: *what? which? who? whom? whose?*
What is her name? Which of you is Sara?

TIP 73 Pronoun: relative
The majority of these are the same as interrogative pronouns, but they're used
differently: *that, which, who, whom, whose*

1. **'Who', 'whom' and 'whose' refer to people; 'which' to things; and 'that' to**
things or people: *"A critic is a man who knows the way but can't drive the car."*
[Kenneth Tynan] *This is the book which I recommended. This is the book that I*
recommended. Is this the woman that you spoke to yesterday?

2. **'Who', 'which' or 'that' can be used with animals. If you know the name of the**
animal, you can use 'who': *Thomas is the cat who terrorises the other cats. Thomas is*
the cat which terrorises the other cats. Thomas is the cat that terrorises the other cats.

3. **Don't use 'which' with people:** *The girl which I saw at the library…* ✗
Write or say: *The girl whom I saw at the library…* ✓

4. **With a superlative structure (TIP 51), you must use 'that':**
It was the fastest race that he had ever run. ✓

Note

In such sentences as the one above, you can omit 'that': *It was the*
fastest race he had ever run.

If you do this, your spellchecker may remind you to put in 'that' before
'he'. Whether you do so or not is a matter of choice and style. I tend to
put it in.

TIP 74
Pronoun: the worst mistake (Advanced Point)
The worst mistake you can make with pronouns (and adjectives) is to use the
plural 'they', 'their' and 'them' instead of the singular 'he', 'she', 'him' or 'her'.

I'm not sure if this is through laziness or ignorance – but it leads to some very odd sentences, such as: *Every nurse must wash their* (adjective) *hands after each patient.* ✗ *The woman does not have to reveal the fact that they* (personal pronoun) *are pregnant.* ✗

Not too difficult to rewrite correctly. Try yourself before checking below. There is more than one way: *Every nurse must wash his or her* (adjective) *hands after each patient.* ✓ *All nurses must wash their hands after each patient.* ✓ *The person concerned does not have to reveal the fact that she* (personal pronoun) *is pregnant.* ✓ *The women do not have to reveal the fact that they* (personal pronoun) *are pregnant.* ✓

Note

The possessive pronoun and adjective 'theirs' is used sometimes for 'his' or 'hers': *Your car is a BMW; theirs* (pronoun) *is a Toyota.* (Fine, if it belongs to two people; otherwise state if it's 'his' or 'hers'.) *One of the parents lost their* (adjective) *camera.* ✗ Correct this.

To prevent this error, use 'his' and 'her', or make the subject plural to use 'their': *Has everyone taken his or her ticket?* ✓ *Have all of them taken their tickets?* ✓

TIP 75 Pronoun: indefinite

These are pronouns that replace nouns:
Singular: *another, anybody, anyone, anything, each, either, everybody, everyone, everything, neither, nobody, no one, nothing, one, other, somebody, someone, something*
Plural: *both, few, many, others, several*
Singular or plural: *all, any, more, most, none, some*

1. **Singular indefinite pronouns take singular verbs:** *No one is lost.*

2. **Plural indefinite pronouns take plural verbs:** *Many of the players were early.*

3. **For indefinite pronouns that can be either singular or plural, it depends on what the indefinite pronoun refers to:** *Most of the players were early.*
Most of the grass was brown.

TIP 76 Conjunction

Conjunctions join words or other constructions. What are called co-ordinating conjugations include 'and', 'or' and 'but'. Subordinating conjunctions are words like 'if', 'unless', 'because', 'although', 'when'.

Remember that a road junction joins roads. **A conjunction joins words or groups of words (when these are grammatical equivalents).**

Some of the most important conjunctions are: *although, and, as, because, but, for, if, nor, or, so, when, yet*

Conjunctions can join:

1. **Two nouns:** *salt and pepper*

2. **Two verbs:** *shaken but not stirred*

3. **Two pronouns:** *she and I*

4. **Two phrases:** *in the sea or on the beach*

5. **Two sentences:** *"He knows nothing; and he thinks he knows everything. That points clearly to a political career."* [George Bernard Shaw] (The third sentence is irrelevant as regards the point being illustrated. But to omit it would be to deny you the point of the other two!)

TIP 77 Preposition
A preposition is a word or a group of words placed in front of a noun, pronoun or phrase. For example, in the sentence, *The cat sleeps in the basket*, the word 'in' is a preposition, introducing the prepositional phrase 'in the basket'.

Let's see how prepositions change the meaning of a sentence entirely:
They ran along the path, into the wood and over the hill.
They ran up the path, through the wood and down the hill.

Here are some examples of prepositions: *aboard, about, above, across, after, among, apart from, around, at, before, behind, below, between, beyond, by, by means of, considering, down, during, except, for, from, in, in addition to, in front of, of, on, on account of, onto, opposite, out of, outside, over, owing to, past, regarding, since, through, to, towards, under, until, up, upon, with, without*

You'll notice that some prepositions are made up of two or more words:
apart from, on account of.

TIP 78 Prepositional phrase
A prepositional phrase is made up of a preposition and the words following it:
because of the weather, underneath the table, owing to the rise in prices

TIP 79 Preposition: and other parts of speech
Many people aren't sure of the difference between a conjunction, an adverb and a preposition. The work they do in a sentence is entirely different:
across (preposition) *the road*
We shall soon be across (adverb)
for (preposition) *himself*
What's it all for (adverb)?

After (conjunction) *he had finished the book, he returned it to the library.*
Soon after (adverb), *they emigrated.*

So, remember that some words are not automatically one particular part of speech. Think about what work a word is doing in a particular sentence. If *you* don't know, your dictionary does.

TIP 80 Exclamation
An exclamation or interjection is an emotional utterance, which may or may not be a full sentence. It's one or more words expressing surprise or some other feeling, and it nearly always has an exclamation mark after it.
That's all! Wow! Hi! Whoops! In your dreams! Well done!

They have no grammatical function – what more could one ask? You'll probably use an exclamation mark, but in no circumstances should you use more than one – as here – poor style!!!

TIP 81 Sentence: what is it?
1. A sentence begins with a capital letter and ends with a full stop, question mark or exclamation mark. A sentence is a group of words which makes complete sense.

All writing is made up of sentences, so the way *you* write sentences defines your own style.

Knowing how a correct sentence works, you can then choose, on rare occasions, *not* to write one. It's not essential to write complete sentences all the time. However, you need to be very sure of yourself before you choose to write what are known as 'sentence fragments'. See 'choose to'? There's a great deal of difference between sentence fragments that are deliberate and those that are accidental – and wrong. Your spellchecker knows about sentence fragments and will remind you when you've written one.

2. The most basic type of sentence is as follows:

Subject	**Verb**	**Object**
The man	*ate*	*the apple.*
She	*touched*	*her hair.*

3. How many words are there in the shortest sentence? One (provided that it's a command): *Run! Help!*

Here you imagine, but don't say/write, the word(s) 'you (must)'. 'You' would be the subject of the verbs above.

Usually, a sentence has a minimum of two words: *Dogs bark. I sleep. We work.*

Work out which is the subject and which the verb in the examples above.

If you can remember the rule about a sentence being a group of words (two or mostly more) with a SUBJECT (noun or pronoun) and a FINITE VERB, you *cannot* write an incorrect sentence.

Read the last sentence again, and make sure that you understand and will remember it! It's one of the most important things you'll learn from this book!

TIP 82 Sentence: the four types
The four types of sentences are: statement, command, question and exclamation.

1. **The most common sentence is a statement:** *"Mr. [Henry] James writes fiction as if it were a painful duty."* [Oscar Wilde]

2. **A question or interrogatory sentence:** *How do you do?*

3. **A command or imperative:** *"Read over your compositions, and wherever you meet a passage which you think is particularly fine, strike it out."* [Samuel Johnson]

4. **An exclamation:** *What a good pianist Penny is!*

Note the punctuation used in these sentences.

TIP 83 Sentence: simple
A simple sentence has one finite verb: *The cat sat on the mat* ('cat' subject, 'sat' verb, in the past tense).

As you know, a sentence must have a subject and a finite verb. Do you remember that a finite verb is one which has a tense? Good!

Is this a sentence? *Oliver, being my eldest grandchild…*

No, because, although there is a verb, 'being', this verb is *not* finite. It's a present participle, and the sentence is incomplete. It has no main verb.

Here are examples of two simple sentences of different lengths: *She ran away.*
I have no idea why she did this, but can only assume it was because she was unhappy in the institution in which she had been placed at a very young age.

Now, find the subjects and verbs.

TIP 84 Sentence: clauses
Before we go on to other types of sentences, let's look for a moment at clauses. Anything other than a simple sentence (which only has one main clause) has at least two, each with its own subject and finite verb.

This sentence has one main clause and is a simple sentence:
The cat walked into the kitchen.

If clauses are added to this sentence, they are called 'subordinate' or 'dependent' clauses, because they depend on the main clause and are not sentences in their own right: *The cat walked into the kitchen because it was hungry.*

Two clauses now, a main one and a subordinate clause: 'because it was hungry'.
All sentences are built up in this way.

TIP 85 Sentence: compound
Compound sentences have two main verbs, so have two main clauses joined with a conjunction, often 'and', 'or', or 'but'. The subject may be the same in both clauses, or there may be two different subjects:
Have you got time, or do you have to go now? The rain fell, but the party continued.

The comma before the conjunction is optional. It tends to be used more in AmE than in BrE.

TIP 86 Sentence: complex (Advanced Point)
A complex sentence has a main clause and a subordinate or dependent clause.

A subordinate clause is usually introduced by a conjunction, and is often divided from the main clause with a comma.

The subordinate clause could be removed, and a correct sentence would remain. However, the reverse would not be true. So:
When advertising is persuasive, people often buy.

Which part of these could stand on its own as a simple sentence? Yes, of course, the second part. So, you can see that the main clause doesn't have to be the first clause.

Let's look at some in which the main clause comes first: *They went home when the meeting was over. She studied for ten years so that she could become a doctor.*

Now, two more. Work out which is the main and which the subordinate or dependent clause: *Your writing of sentences will improve after you learn how clauses work.*

TIP 87 Sentence: compound-complex (Advanced Point)
A compound-complex sentence has two main clauses plus at least one subordinate clause. Can you work out which is which in this example? *She had hoped to go to Paris, but was prevented from going because she had a car accident.*

The two main clauses are 'She had hoped to go to Paris' and 'but (she) was prevented from going', and the dependent clause is 'because she had a car accident'.

Look at a few other sentences and see whether you can analyse them into clauses. **This will help you to write your own correct sentences.**

TIP 88 Run-on sentences

Many people seem to have no idea where one sentence ends and another one begins, they just keep on writing, they may put in a comma but they seem to have forgotten how to use a full stop, you can now see that this is a good example of what I'm talking about, and if you didn't notice before now, perhaps you're one of those whose sentences are as long as paragraphs.

Before correcting this, how many sentences do you think the 'sentence' above contains? Probably four. Let's improve it.

Many people seem to have no idea where one sentence ends and another one begins. They just keep on writing. They may put in a comma, but they seem to have forgotten how to use a full stop. You can now see that this is a good example of what I'm talking about, and, if you didn't notice before now, perhaps you're one of those who write sentences as long as paragraphs.

I said probably four, as you could join sentences one and two, not with a comma, but with a colon, and/or you could split the last sentence into two. Try! Make small changes if you need to.

How do you know when to stop one sentence and start another? The easy answer is that you write one statement and then put a full stop, in other words, just one idea to a sentence. Or, you count the words and stop if your 'sentence' is longer than 17-20 words. Or, you could read it aloud and stop when you get out of breath (not the best suggestion, as you may take this as a challenge!). Then you write another statement. As above, sentences can be joined by colons or semicolons where appropriate, but they can't just run on willy-nilly with commas. Look out for examples of this mistake.

TIP 89 Sentence: negatives

The most important negatives are 'no' and 'not': *There is no cake left.*
I'm not going to do any more work today.

Others include neither, nor, never, none, nobody, nothing, nowhere.

Two negatives make a positive: *She didn't want no sandwiches.* ✗ (This means she did want some.) *She didn't want any sandwiches.* ✓

But if you put a negative word such as 'no' at the beginning of a sentence, you can use a second negative without turning your sentence into a positive:
No, she didn't want any sandwiches.

'Barely', 'hardly' and 'scarcely' are kinds of negatives, so should not be used with a second negative: *She hadn't scarcely any friends.* ✗ *She had scarcely any friends.* ✓

Note

> If you start a sentence with one of these words, the normal word order of subject and verb is inverted (reversed): *Barely had she arrived when her mother began to prepare a large meal. Hardly had Helen finished her meal when her grandchildren arrived.*

TIP 90 Phrase

A phrase is a group of at least two words which doesn't make complete sense. It doesn't have a finite verb and doesn't express a complete thought:
under a low bridge, in the river, from Poland, by reading a lot

You can use a phrase as part of a sentence but not alone. An opening phrase requires a comma before the first clause: *By reading a lot, you will improve your English.*

Unit 1: Review

Look up the answers on Pages 150-151, or use a dictionary and the Internet if you wish. No one is asking you to remember everything: we all have to look things up in the appropriate place. It's when people *think* they know and don't bother to check that mistakes occur.

There may be occasions where what you've written may not be identical to the answer given, but I'm sure you have the intelligence to work out whether your answer means the same.

You may find some of the questions easy – good! That means you know the particular point. The only difference between something which is easy and something which is difficult is whether you know it or not.

Good luck!

1. How many parts of speech are there?
2. Is 'the' the definite or the indefinite article?
3. Would you put 'a' or 'an' in front of 'hour'?
4. What is a noun?
5. Which kind of noun requires a capital letter?
6. Which of them describes something that isn't touchable?
7. 'Herd' is an example of which kind of noun?
8. What is a countable noun? Give an example.
9. Is 'advice' a countable noun?
10. What is a suffix?
11. What is a verb?

12. What are the three main tenses of verbs?
13. Is 'talk' a regular or an irregular verb?
14. Is 'swim' a regular or an irregular verb?
15. What is the most important verb in a sentence called?
16. What are the three main helping or 'auxiliary' verbs?
17. *She did that well, didn't she?* What is the grammatical name for the last part of that sentence?
18. What is the main use of 'shall' and 'will'?
19. Is this correct? *Can I go now, please?*
20. *If he can eat less, he would be thinner.* Is this correct?
21. How do you define the subject of a verb?
22. How do you find the subject of a sentence?
23. *A new set of rules are coming into operation.* Correct this sentence.
24. What are the three parts of a basic sentence?
25. *For the holiday, she bought new clothes, new shoes, and a new suitcase.* Write down the objects in this sentence.
26. *She hesitated and then decided.* Are the verbs in this sentence transitive or intransitive?
27. *She felt unwell.* What kind of verb is this?
28. What is the plural form of the first person?
29. *To decide; to hope; to spend.* What are these?
30. Is this verb active or passive? *She played tennis every day.*
31. Should you say *if I were you* or *if I was you?*
32. What are these? *Talking, moving, hoping.*
33. Do you need inverted commas for indirect speech?
34. Put this sentence into direct speech. *She asked if he could come.*
35. Is this correct? *Either John or Patrick have to drive.*
36. *Each was hoping he would be chosen.* Is this right?
37. What is the adjective's main role?
38. In what two positions could you find adjectives?
39. Are 'a' and 'the' adjectives?
40. Put these adjectives in order. *(She wanted) a pink bright furry large toy.*
41. Now punctuate 40 correctly.
42. What are the three degrees of comparison for adjectives?
43. Write the three degrees of comparison for 'big'.
44. Now the three degrees of comparison for 'good'.
45. Is this correct? *I do like those kind of books.*
46. What kind of adjective is this? *My book.*
47. *For each person who said yes, eight said no.* Is this correct?
48. Is this correct? *I haven't got any money.*
49. Can you say: *The girl was more happier than she had ever been?*
50. What three things do adverbs tell you about a verb?
51. What are the three degrees of comparison of 'badly'?
52. Is this correct? *However the train did arrive on time.*
53. Adverbs can modify verbs, adjectives and what else?
54. *Drive careful.* Is this correct?

55. What is a pronoun?
56. Give an example.
57. Is this right? *The prizes were won by he and I.*
58. *The man who was driving was my uncle.* Is this correct?
59. Correct this: *Everyone waited their turn.*
60. What is a conjunction?
61. Which are the two most common conjunctions?
62. What is a preposition?
63. What is an exclamation? Give an example.
64. Why is it wrong to use more than one exclamation mark?
65. What is a sentence?
66. What is the most basic type of sentence?
67. How many words are in the shortest sentence?
68. What are the four types of sentence?
69. Define a simple sentence.
70. What is a subordinate clause?
71. What type of sentence is this? *I arrived on time, but my sister was late.*
72. Define a complex sentence.
73. This is a run-on sentence. Correct it (there could be more than one way, so mark yourself as you deem fit!). *I have been writing this list of questions for two hours now it's very difficult especially as I want to test you before and after you have studied the grammar concerned and I don't want to make the questions too difficult or too easy I hope that I have succeeded and that the marks add up to 100.*
74. Is this correct? *I don't want to write no more sentences.*
75. What is a phrase? Give an example.

Unit 2: Common Errors

"Errors look so very ugly."
George Eliot

You'll find the following are mostly listed in pairs which are sometimes confused (you may see a reminder such 'Commonly Confused Words' when you spellcheck your work for such words). Many you will already know. Choose to learn whichever you think will be useful for you. Some of the words have second or more meanings in addition to those I give below, so you may be aware of different uses.

TIP 91 Accept or Except
These are two very different words and must not be confused.

'Accept' means 'to receive' or 'to agree to': *She accepted the invitation to the party. She accepts that she is not a great singer.*
You're more likely to come across 'except' as a preposition meaning 'apart from' or 'leaving out': *It rained every day last week except Tuesday.*

The verb meaning 'to leave out', is very rarely used, and the likelihood is, if you do need a verb, it will be 'accept'. Here's an example anyway:
I except all cyclists from my last remark.

TIP 92 Advance or Advanced (Advanced Point)
Although 'advance' can be a verb, let's look at it here as an adjective. The mistake comes when the second word is used for the first.

'Advance' means 'ahead in time or place': *Advance bookings here.* ✔
Advance Warning: there will be no trains on December 25. ✔

What you may see is: *Advanced bookings here.* ✘
Advanced Warning: there will be no trains on December 25. ✘

'Advanced' means 'above a standard level': *Advanced Level examinations require diligent study. She was an advanced student of Portuguese.*

TIP 93 Advice or Advise
Remember that 'advice' is a noun and 'advise' is a verb:
Her advice was that I should go to bed earlier. She advised me to go to bed earlier.

When confronted at any time with 'practice' (noun) and 'practise' (verb); or 'licence' (noun) and 'license' (verb), think of 'advice' and 'advise', where the spelling and sound are different for the noun and the verb, and then apply the

same logic to the other two – where there's no difference in sound to help you. (See also TIP 189 on Practice or Practise.)

N.B. In the Unites States, 'practice' and 'license' are used for both noun and verb.

 In the UK, purists (including me) prefer 'adviser' to 'advisor' – though you will see both.

TIP 94 Affect or Effect
These may both be verbs:
To 'affect' means to 'produce an effect upon': *Working long hours doesn't affect me.*
To 'effect' means 'to bring about or to accomplish': *The new chairman effected changes in all departments.*

You're more likely to meet 'effect' as a noun than as a verb:
The treatment had an amazing effect on the child.

TIP 95 Aggravate or Annoy
These are not interchangeable. The first means 'to make worse' and the second is what you think it is: *She aggravated the wound by scratching it.* ✔ *She was aggravated by the irritating child.* ✘ *She was annoyed by the irritating child.* ✔

TIP 96 Agree To or Agree With
You 'agree to' a proposition and 'agree with' a person: *I agreed to the suggestion of leaving early. I agreed with her that leaving early was a good idea.*

 TIP 97
Allow or Enable
'Allow' is frequently used for 'enable'. These two verbs should *not* be confused, as they *don't* mean the same thing. **To prevent yourself from making this mistake, remember...**

'Allow' means 'to give permission': *She would not allow me to wear my new shoes.* ✔
'Enable' means 'to make possible': *The website enabled the company to reach more customers.* ✔

What you may see is: *The website allowed the company to reach more customers.* ✘

This point isn't difficult once you remember the meanings of the two verbs – but it is a very common error.

TIP 98 Allowed or Aloud
'Allowed' is the past tense of the verb 'allow': *She allowed me to look at all her old photographs.*
'Aloud' is an adverb meaning 'capable of being heard': *He read the poem aloud.*

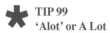 **TIP 99**
'Alot' or A Lot
Contrary to popular belief, 'alot' is an erroneous fictional word, much used.

Why is this word used? Ignorance, I'm afraid. Just try to work it out. 'A' (indefinite article) plus 'lot' (abstract noun) is fine, but 'alot'? You won't find this in your dictionary or spellchecker.

'A lot' (*always* **two words) means 'much' or 'many':**
She bought a lot of books for college. He ate a lot of sandwiches.

In any case, 'a lot' is informal, so should be used only where appropriate.

TIP 100 Already or All Ready
Throughout this Unit, you'll be shown words where there are two versions, one as one word, and another where the one word is split into two, as here. Both can be correct in context. As you read these, you'll begin to work out how not to make such mistakes in the future – just the small matter of thinking.

'Already' (adverb) **means 'by now' or 'by then':**
By the time the last note had died away, the audience was already clapping.
'All ready' means 'all of us/all of them etc. are or were ready':
The children were all ready for the party.

Now, not very stylish, but to prove it can be done, both together:
Already, the firemen were all ready.

TIP 101 Alright or All Right
Which do *you* use? Maybe whichever you use is acceptable, as 'alright' is creeping towards recognition.

Is it ever all right to use 'alright'? No, when writing formally, always use 'all right'. It's better here to err on the safe side.

TIP 102 Alternate or Alternative
'Alternate' (adjective) **means 'each in turn'.** It can also be a verb. *She knitted alternate* (adjective) *rows in red and black. He alternated* (verb) *between hope and fear.*
'Alternative' (noun) **means 'any one of two or more possibilities':**
They were left with no alternative but to accept the offer.

Work out the adverbs 'alternately' and 'alternatively' for yourself.

TIP 103 Altogether or All Together
'Altogether' (adverb) **means 'in all' or 'in total':**
There were 15 guests altogether. Altogether, the children consumed 12 hot dogs.
'All together' means that 'all of us etc. are/were together':
The 15 guests were all together in the garden.

TIP 104 Always or All Ways
'Always' is an adverb meaning 'at all times', 'often': *They are always complaining.*
'All ways' is simply 'all' plus 'ways': *We tried all ways to make her join in.*

TIP 105
Among or Between
Do you know the difference between the two? It's a *very* common error to use the wrong word.

'Between' is used with *two* things or people:
He had to choose between learning French or German.
'Among' is used with *three or more* things or people:
He shared his birthday cake among all his colleagues.

See TIP 120 for 'Between you and me'.

TIP 106 Amoral or Immoral
'Amoral' (adjective) **means 'not concerned with morals or 'having no moral principles':** *Birds are amoral.*
'Immoral' (adjective) **means 'morally wrong':** *It's immoral to steal.*

TIP 107
Amount or Number
The following may look correct, but are not: *A large amount of my friends came to the party.* ✘ *I saw a large amount of rare birds on my recent holiday.* ✘

Let's put them right: *A large number of my friends came to the party.* ✔ *I saw a large number of rare birds on my recent holiday.* ✔

Do you remember countable and uncountable nouns?
'Amount' can only refer to *uncountable* nouns: *We ate a large amount of food at Christmas.* ✔
'Number' refers to *countable* nouns: *A large number of animals has become extinct.* ✔

Look now at **Fewer or Less** (TIP 161) to see how these four words interrelate.

TIP 108 Ancestor or Antecedent
'Ancestor' is a person who goes before.
'Antecedent' is something which goes before.

Don't confuse these, as in the report I read in a national newspaper, where mention was made of fishermen whose antecedents had been fishing certain seas for centuries. Use 'ancestor' here.

TIP 109 Anymore or Any More
'Anymore' is an invented word. Just stick to 'any more'. *I couldn't eat anymore chocolates.* ✘ *I couldn't eat any more chocolates.* ✔

TIP 110 Anyone or Any One
'Anyone' means 'any person': *Anyone might have done it.*
'Any one' means 'any single one': *Any one of the three suspects could have stolen the statue.*

TIP 111 Anytime or Any Time
'Anytime' is another word that is not in the dictionary.
Use 'any time': *You can work any time you like.*

TIP 112 Anyway or Any Way
'Anyway' (adverb) **means 'at any rate':** *Anyway, I told you it wouldn't be easy.*

Note the comma after the introductory adverb.

'Any' is an adjective plus 'way', a noun:
Any way you look at the problem, it won't be easy to solve.

TIP 113 Apart or A Part
'Apart' is an adverb meaning 'separately' or 'excepting':
Apart from one small boy, all the others had left.
'A part' is just a part of the whole: *We watched a part of the play in rehearsal.*

I have seen: *You will be apart of the team.* ✗
This writer clearly did not think.

So, before you write any word beginning with 'a', work out which one you're actually using:

around	or	*a round*
asleep	or	*a sleep*
away	or	*a way*
awake	or	*a wake*
awhile	or	*a while*

All of these are correct – in context.

TIP 114 Are or Our
I once received an email stating: "*I am writing to enquire if you have had any problems using are software?*"
'Are' is a plural part of the verb 'to be':
We are hoping to go to New Zealand next year.
'Our' is a possessive adjective meaning 'belonging to us'. That is what should have been used: *I am writing to enquire if you have had any problems using our software.*

I have also removed the question mark since this is an indirect question, which doesn't require a question mark.

TIP 115 Assure, Ensure or Insure
You 'assure' your life.
To 'ensure' means 'to make certain'.
You 'insure' against risk.

'Assure' can also mean 'to make someone sure':
I assure you that your English is getting better every day!

TIP 116 Avoid or Prevent
Another two words frequently misused.
To 'avoid' means to 'keep or get away from': *He avoided arrest by escaping to Spain.*
To 'prevent' means to 'stop from happening':
Regular visits to the dentist can help to prevent tooth decay.

Practice helps on this one. Listen for it and try to decide if the correct word has been used – often it hasn't.

TIP 117 Bad or Badly
'Bad' is an adjective, so it qualifies a noun or a pronoun: *He had a bad headache.* ✔
'Badly' is an adverb, so modifies a verb: *She reacted badly to the suggestion.* ✔

Don't write or say: *I didn't know things were going so bad.* ✘

TIP 118 Because after Reason
'Because' means 'for the reason that'. You shouldn't write: *The reason for her success was because she trained every day.* ✘ Write: *The reason for her success was that she trained every day.* ✔ Or: *Her success came because she trained every day.* ✔

TIP 119 Beside or Besides
'Beside' means next to: *He was sitting beside his friend.*
'Besides' means 'in addition to':
Besides his friend, there were three other people present.

TIP 120
Between You and Me
How often have you heard 'between you and I'? What's wrong with this? The reason it is wrong is that a preposition is followed by an *object pronoun*, such as 'me', 'him', 'her', 'them'. 'I' is a *subject* pronoun.
So, the following is correct, and *nothing* else is: *between you and me*
Keep repeating to yourself: 'between you and me'.

TIP 121 Biannual or Biennial
'Biennial' is every two years.
'Biannual' is twice a year.

TIP 122 Board or Bored
Not difficult – just think!

"...he was carried on a board while asleep." [David Hume]
Some children get bored easily.

TIP 123 Brake or Break
Without a brake, your car would be illegal.
And an example for break:
"Break, break, break, / On thy cold grey stones, O Sea!" [Alfred, Lord Tennyson]

TIP 124 Breach or Breech
'Breach' is a breaking of, e.g., a promise, a contract or a fortification:
The motorist breached the law when he parked illegally.
'Breech' can be used to describe the position of a baby at or before birth, where the legs present first, rather than the head.

TIP 125 Breath or Breathe
'Breath' (noun) rhymes with 'Beth', while 'breathe' rhymes with 'seethe'. Just remember that.

Everyone can spell 'breath', but some people wrongly use this word for the verb as well: *He couldn't breath.* ✗

Let's put this right: *He couldn't breathe.* ✓

TIP 126 Buy, By or 'Bye
'Buy' is a verb: *She decided to buy a new car.*
'By' is a preposition, adverb or noun, here a preposition: *by the stream*
''Bye' is a colloquial English abbreviation for 'goodbye'.

TIP 127 Canvas or Canvass
'Canvas' is coarse cloth.
To 'canvass' is to solicit votes for e.g., an election candidate.

TIP 128 Caster or Castor
'Caster' describes a fine type of sugar.
A 'castor' is a wheel on the bottom of a chair.

TIP 129 Cereal or Serial
You might eat your cereal while watching a serial on television.

TIP 130 Childish or Childlike
'Childish' is often used derogatively, e.g. of the behaviour of adults.
'Childlike' means having the good qualities of a child, e.g. innocence.

TIP 131 Chord or Cord
A musical 'chord' is a combination of usually three or more notes played together. A 'cord' is a rope or a part of the body, e.g. spinal cord.

TIP 132 Classic, Classical or Classics (Advanced Point)
'Classic' (adjective) **means 'of the first class', 'remarkably typical':**
She was wearing a classic two-piece suit.
'Classical' means 'serious' or 'conventional': *Classical music is the delight of many.*
Classics comprises the languages, literature, culture etc. of the ancient Greeks and Romans: *She studied Classics at Oxford.*

TIP 133 Coarse or Course
'Coarse' means 'crude' or 'rough in texture':
The monk's habit was made of coarse cloth.
'Course' is a noun and a verb. Let's consider just the noun, 'a series of lessons in a particular subject': *She was studying an English language course.*

TIP 134 Compare To or Compare With
'Compare to' means 'to liken one thing/person to another':
The bank compared last year's figures to this year's.
'Compare with' means 'to make a relative assessment', to show similarities or differences: *I compared this year's results with last year's.*

TIP 135 Complement or Compliment
'Complement' (verb or noun) **means 'something that completes':**
The scarf complemented her coat.
'Compliment' (verb or noun) **is a word or two of praise, or a formal greeting:**
She was complimented (verb) *on the beautiful flower arrangement.*

Note that you compliment someone 'on', not 'for' something.

TIP 136 Confidant or Confident
'Confidant(e)' (noun) **is a person one can entrust with secrets.**
'Confident' is an adjective meaning 'bold', 'self-assured'.

TIP 137 Continual(ly) or Continuous(ly)
This is another one which can give difficulty.
'Continual' implies something happens regularly:
The telephone rang continually (frequently recurring).
'Continuously' means without intermission or interruption:
It rained continuously for two days (the rain did not stop).

TIP 138 Currant or Current
A currant (noun) **is a small dried seedless fruit:** *I like sultanas but I dislike currants.*
'Current' can be a noun or an adjective:
Tony's current (adjective) *project was writing a book of poetry. The current* (noun) *had an undertow, and he feared he might be drowned.*

TIP 139 Defective or Deficient
'Defective' (adjective) **means 'faulty in quality':** *The computer was defective.*
'Deficient' (adjective) **means 'lacking in something':** *Her body was deficient in iron.*

TIP 140 Delusion or Illusion
'Delusion' (noun) **indicates a false assumption:**
She was under the delusion that her son was a genius.
An 'illusion' (noun) **is a distortion of the senses:**
He confidently assumes that he will win the race, but this is just an illusion.

TIP 141 Dependant or Dependent (Advanced Point)
'Dependant' is a noun meaning 'someone who relies on another':
The wealthy entrepreneur suddenly found that he had many dependants.
'Dependent' is an adjective (usually followed by 'on') meaning 'unable to do without': *The homeless man was dependent on charity.*

TIP 142 Desert or Dessert
In the first example, the accent is on the first syllable; in the second, it's on the second:
The Sahara Desert is reputed to be the hottest and largest in the world.
For dessert, she chose fruit.
'Desert' can also be an adjective, as in 'desert island'.

There is also a verb 'to desert': *It is unlikely that a bird would desert its young.*

TIP 143 Die or Dye
We shall all die one day.
We don't all choose to dye our hair.

The present participle is 'dying' for the first and 'dyeing' for the second.

TIP 144 Different From, To or Than
'Different from' is Standard English: *Every day is different from the next.*
'Different to' is frequently used.

If you're writing formally, my advice is to use 'different from'.

The verb is 'to differ from'. But you can be 'indifferent to'!

TIP 145 Direct or Directly (Advanced Point)
'Direct' can be used as an adjective, an adverb or a verb:
Which is the most direct (adjective) *route to Moscow? We flew direct* (adverb) *to Boston. Could you direct* (verb) *me to the station, please?*

Don't write: *We flew directly to Boston.* ✘
Unless you mean: *We flew immediately to Boston.* ✔

'Directly' (adverb) **means 'at once', 'immediately', 'exactly', etc.:**
They live directly opposite the church.

Can you see what's wrong with the following?
Plus a consultation with the author directly. ✗

To put this right: *Plus a consultation with the author direct.* ✔

TIP 146 Disinterested or Uninterested (Advanced Point)
Some see the prefix 'dis' implying negation, so assume that 'disinterested' is the opposite of 'interested'. It isn't.

'Disinterested' (adjective) **means 'impartial' or 'unbiased' (with no personal interest):** *A tennis umpire is disinterested.* (He doesn't take sides.)
'Uninterested' (adjective) **means 'to have no interest in':** *Jack's daughter was disinterested in football.* ✗ *Jack's daughter was uninterested in football.* ✔

TIP 147 Draft or Draught
The first noun, 'draft', refers to making a rough or first copy:
She made the first draft of her book several years before publication.
'Draught' is a current of air: *He could feel the draught coming from under the door.*

TIP 148 Due To or Owing To (Advanced Point)
'Due to' means 'caused by'. It is followed by a noun or pronoun. If you can't substitute 'caused by', don't use this:
Her spots were due to her diet. Her spots were caused by her diet.
'Owing to' is similar to 'because of': *His early retirement was owing to ill health. His early retirement was because of ill health.*

TIP 149 Eatable or Edible
Both words mean 'capable of being eaten', but 'edible' is used in contexts where there is a possibility of harm to the person who eats the item. The negative forms are 'uneatable' and 'inedible'.

TIP 150 Economic or Economical (Advanced Point)
'Economic' (adjective) **means 'of or relating to economics':**
The economic interests of a country may lead it to act unethically.
'Economical' (adjective) **means 'sparing in the use of resources':**
It isn't economical to buy a small size, when there is a cheaper, larger alternative.

TIP 151 e.g. or i.e.
Do you know the Latin words these initials represent? If not, learn them and you'll never confuse them again.

e.g. (exempli gratia) means 'for example':
There are many different language courses you can choose from, e.g. Spanish, French, German, Italian, Portuguese, Norwegian or Russian.
i.e. (id est) means 'that is':
The nurse had a very early shift the next day, i.e. one starting at five a.m.

TIP 152 Elicit or Illicit
'Elicit' is a verb meaning 'to draw out': *I elicited the fact that he had been here before.*
'Illicit' (adjective) means 'unlawful' or 'forbidden':
Illicit drinking was common during the Prohibition in America.

TIP 153 Emigrate or Immigrate
To 'emigrate' means to leave a country: *My cousin emigrated to Australia;*
to 'immigrate' means to come to live in a country in which you were not born.

TIP 154 Eminent or Imminent (Advanced Point)
'Eminent' means 'distinguished' or 'remarkable': *The eminent judge passed sentence.*
'Imminent' means 'about to happen': *Rain is imminent.*

TIP 155 Enormity or Magnitude (Advanced Point)
'Magnitude' is the rather cumbersome word often required, as this refers to large size; whereas 'enormity' means extreme wickedness and is often incorrectly used, as here: *Captain Lloyd explained the enormity of the task facing his men.* ✗

Now, a correct example with 'enormity': *The man did not seem to comprehend the enormity of his crime.* ✓

TIP 156 Envelop or Envelope
'Envelop' is a verb meaning to wrap up or cover completely:
The child was enveloped in his mother's arms.

The other you'll know:
"Good news rarely comes in a brown envelope." [Henry d'Avigdor-Goldsmid]

TIP 157 Etc. or 'Ect.'
'Etc.' is an abbreviation of 'et cetera', the Latin for 'and the rest':
Last year, I grew thyme, basil, sage, rosemary, etc.

'Ect.' is another word which does *not* exist. It's a misspelling by those who don't know the Latin origin. Tip: it may help you to think of another language, where 'et' or similar means 'and'.

TIP 158 Everyday or Every Day
The usual mistake is to use 'everyday' for 'every day'. This is an example of either being ignorant of the fact that there are two ways of using the same words, or lack of thought as to which one to select.

Everyday: *The bank opens at nine everyday.* ✗ *The bank opens at nine every day.* ✓
Cleaning one's teeth is an everyday (adjective) *routine.* ✓

TIP 159 Everyone or Every One
'Everyone' means every person: *Not everyone has been to Paris.*
'Every one' means 'every single one':
Have you really read every one of Shakespeare's plays?

And an artificially contrived example of both in one sentence:
Not everyone has seen every one of the latest films.

TIP 160 Farther or Further (Advanced Point)
'Farther' and 'further' are both comparatives of far (referring to distance):
New York is further/farther away from Madrid than London is.

'Further' (adjective, adverb) **can mean 'to a greater extent', 'in addition to', 'until changed', etc.** It may refer to amount or time: *You should check this point further* (adverb). *This school is closed until further* (adjective) *notice.*

There is also a verb, 'to further': *She furthered her career by taking extra courses.*

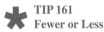

TIP 161
Fewer or Less
Do you remember **Amount or Number** (TIP 107)?

'Fewer' is used when the number of things can be counted. 'Fewer' links with 'number': *There are fewer chocolates in this box than there were last night!*

'Less' is used when the number of things or qualities *cannot* be counted. 'Less' links with 'amount': *I have less need of money now than I had twenty years ago.*

Confusing these two is very common, usually by saying 'less' for 'fewer' rather than the other way round. A rough guide, if you're not sure, is to use 'less' with singular nouns (less food, less money) and 'fewer' with plural nouns (fewer leaves, fewer books).

TIP 162 Forever or For Ever
Another pair used without any thought. Again, they aren't interchangeable.
'Forever' is an adverb meaning 'continually', or 'persistently':
The dog was forever pestering me to take him for a walk.
'For ever' means 'for all time': *The journey seemed to go on for ever.*

The incorrect tendency is to use 'forever' when 'for ever' is required.

TIP 163 Formally or Formerly
'Formally' is how one is expected to dress, speak, write, etc. on certain occasions: *You are requested to reply formally.*
'Formerly' means 'in the past': *Formerly, she was a gardener.*

TIP 164 Hear or Here
Too easy really: ***Come over here so that you can hear better.***

TIP 165 Historic or Historical (Advanced Point)
'Historic' means 'having some importance in history', usually referring to a person or an event: *The Declaration of Independence was a historic document.*
'Historical' means 'having to do with history' or 'from the past': *The Declaration of Independence has great historical significance.*

'Historically' is the adverbial form of both words.

TIP 166
I or Me
A mistake such as: *He drove Jim and I to town* should sound wrong to you. It's unlikely to have happened without a first object, 'Jim' and the word 'and'. Remove 'Jim and', and then read the sentence aloud: 'He drove I to town.' How does it sound? Right? No!

Let's look at another: *Steve bought Jeremy and I some DVDs.* ✗

Would you say 'Steve bought I some DVDs?' I imagine not.

Two warning signs for this error are: 1) a first object, and 2) the word 'and'.
Steve bought Jeremy (first object) *and I some DVDs.* ✗

Here's a second way to check. Repeat the first part of the sentence and you can't go wrong: *He drove Jim and (he drove) me to town.* ✔
Steve bought Jeremy and (he bought) me some DVDs. ✔

TIP 167 Imply or Infer (Advanced Point)
Ask anyone the meaning of these two verbs. Did they know the difference? Read on if *you* don't know.

To 'imply' means to 'say indirectly':
He implied by the expression on his face that he disliked cats.
To 'infer' means to 'draw a conclusion from':
I inferred from his expression that he disliked cats.

In other words, *I* infer and *you/he/she/they* imply.

The mistake is usually using 'infer' for 'imply'. Remember that a speaker implies, whereas a listener infers.

TIP 168 Infamous or Notorious
Two adjectives with similar meanings.
'Infamous' means 'having a bad reputation': *The infamous Al Capone...*
'Notorious' is nastier and means 'well known, especially unfavourably':
The notorious Adolf Hitler...

I once read a letter from a law firm, stating that it was 'notorious for its excellent
results'! I think they meant 'famous' or 'noted'. This is a malapropism (see TIP 332).

TIP 169 Initiate or Instigate
'Initiate' means 'to begin, to get going':
The police initiated an inquiry into the train robbery. ✔
'Instigate' means 'to incite or to persuade someone to do something wrong or bad':
The train robbery was instigated by a notorious bank robber. ✔

So, this kind of thing is wrong, but frequent:
The police instigated an inquiry into the train robbery. ✗

TIP 170 Into or In To, etc. (Advanced Point)
Many prepositions may also be adverbs. This can cause confusion when 'to' follows
'on' or 'in', or when 'on' follows 'up'.

The words 'into', 'onto' and 'upon' followed by an object are prepositions.

The pairs 'in to', 'on to' and 'up on' followed by an object consist of an adverb
followed by a preposition. Their meanings and the grammatical relationships are not the
same as when they are single-word prepositions:
He went into a building. He went in to see his friend.

Can you work out why 'into' is used in the first and 'in to' in the second? Once you can,
you've mastered this point. Try it yourself with 'onto' and 'on to'.

Finally, an improbable beginning of a story:
Once upon a time, there was a horse that stood up on its hind legs.

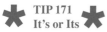
TIP 171
It's or Its
Every intelligent ten-year-old should have mastered this point!

My putting ✱ twice is not a mistake: it's to show you that confusing these two
(*mostly using 'it's' for 'its'*) is the most common error I see. If you learn nothing
else from this whole book, I shall be happy if you *never* make this particular
mistake again!

Let's learn this the easy way first:
1. **All you have to do is to ask yourself: am I writing 'it is' or 'it has' in an**
abbreviated form?

Two simple 'yes' examples: *It's (it has) been raining all day. It's (it is) the best book I've ever read.*

2. If the answer is 'no, I'm not writing "it is" or "it has"', you must write 'its'.
Just learn steps 1 and 2 above, and you'll have mastered the commonest mistake on or off the Internet!

This has been enough instruction for many to stop making this mistake. If you're happy with what you've just learned in steps 1 and 2, go straight to the Note at the end.

For those who are curious to know more, look at how these words break down into grammatical units: **It's: personal pronoun plus verb (contracted form of 'it is' or 'it has'); Its: possessive adjective**

Do you remember that an apostrophe showing possession is only used with a *noun (the computer's memory, Jack's future)*?

Yes? But in case this is still not firmly stuck in your brain...

I repeat: the apostrophe to show possession is only used with NOUNS.

Remembering this will stop you ever putting an apostrophe in 'its' (belonging to it). I repeat: 'its' is a possessive ADJECTIVE.

Note that the error is made far more often this way round:
This printer is the best of it's kind. ✘ *The book is in it's sixth edition.* ✘
This printer is the best of its kind. ✔ *The book is in its sixth edition.* ✔

 Note   Writers both experienced and inexperienced think they're proving that they know that an apostrophe is used where there's some sense of belonging. **Yes, it is; but what they *don't* know is that this is only true of NOUNS!**

I'm going to repeat this simple rule: Ask yourself: **Am I abbreviating 'it is' or 'it has' when I write 'it's'? If not, I must write 'its'.**

I'll leave you with a simple example using both in the same sentence:
Where's the parcel? It's on its way.

Stick this into your brain! Incidentally, the device to use something else to help you remember is called a 'mnemonic' (the first 'm' is silent).

Because it hasn't been mentioned elsewhere, I'll remind you here that there is *never* an apostrophe in any of these other possessive pronouns which end in 's':
yours, hers, ours, theirs

TIP 172 Just and Only (Advanced Point)
The position of these words makes a difference to the meaning of the sentence.

When you use 'just' as an adverb meaning 'only', put it in front of the word it modifies:
Just this shop sells gift vouchers for books. ✓
This shop just sells gift vouchers for books. ✗
This shop sells just gift vouchers for books. ✗
This shop sells gift vouchers just for books. ✓

Similarly, place the word 'only' directly in front of the word it modifies:
Only this shop sells gift vouchers for books. ✓
This shop only sells gift vouchers for books. ✗
This shop sells only gift vouchers for books. ✗
This shop sells gift vouchers only for books. ✓

Work out *exactly* what each of these means; some of them don't make much sense. I've ticked those that could be true.

If you find yourself using 'just' or 'only', stop! Be prepared to move them from where you originally thought they should go – your first thoughts aren't always the best. I know I often move these words around.

Look at this example, where the position of 'just' changes the meaning:
Just give me another week to read this book.

What you could also have said, depending exactly on what you meant, is:
Give me just another week to read this book.

Do you understand the difference?

TIP 173 Later or Latter
These two shouldn't be confused, as they sound different.
'Later' rhymes with 'waiter'; 'latter' rhymes with 'matter'.

'The latter' is often seen in conjunction with 'the former':
Olivia and Lisa bought new dresses. That of the latter (Lisa) *was made of silk, whereas the former's* (Olivia's) *was made of cotton.*

Using 'the latter' prevents repetition of names. Note that 'the latter' is the person or thing you mentioned second, whereas 'the former' is the first-mentioned.

TIP 174
Lay or Lie
'Lay' is a transitive verb, one that takes an object. Since it means 'to place on a surface', you have to lay *something*, you can't just lay somewhere. In addition, it isn't followed by 'on': *She was laying the table.* ✓ *The hens were laying eggs.* ✓

'Lie' is an intransitive verb (one without an object), often followed by 'on' or other preposition, e.g. 'in', 'under': *Peter was lying on the bed.* ✔
The dog lay (past tense of 'lie') *under the table.* ✔

Many people confuse these verbs through ignorance of how they work.

Let's look first at their principal parts:
To lay: 'to place on a surface'

Present	Simple past	Past perfect
lay	*laid*	*(have) laid*

To lie: 'to assume a horizontal position'

Present	Simple past	Past perfect
lie	*lay*	*(have) lain*

Are the meanings the same? Not at all. So, before going on, learn the meanings and the principal parts.

Which is the only word common to both? Yes, 'lay'. But notice that it's the present tense of the first verb, and the past tense of the second.

The most common error is the use of 'lay' and 'laid' for 'lie' and 'lay': *He decided to lay on the bed.* ✘ *He laid on the bed.* ✘ *Whether you choose to lay on a beach in Barbados...* ✘ (From a magazine which prides itself on clear English. I would say this is not clear unless you're a chicken.)

Check with what you've learned above. Can you see why the three examples above are wrong? Now substitute 'lay' with 'lie' in the first, and 'laid' with 'lay' in the second. *He decided to lie on the bed.* ✔ *He lay on the bed.* ✔

I'm sure you don't need me to do the third example for you.

Any better? Until you can say yes – and mean it – you haven't grasped this point. Try them incorrectly as above with your spellchecker. It should warn you about 'Commonly Confused Words'.

Once you understand this point, the next time someone says 'he was laying on the floor', you might like (silently) to wonder *what* he was laying.

Just remember, you can lay a carpet, but you must lie *on* a carpet.

Note
> Finally, 'to lie' meaning 'to tell an untruth'. This is an easy regular verb: *lie, lied, lied*

You're not likely to make mistakes here, but let's just look at it anyway:
He lies all the time to his so-called friends.

TIP 175
Lead or Led

'Lead' (noun) is a metal, and rhymes with 'fed': *The roof was made of lead.*

Also as a noun, rhyming with 'need', 'lead' means something a dog pulls you along by, or 'at the front' (noun, adjective): *The dog tugged at its lead. The Italian runner was in the lead. The lead* (adjective) *guitarist broke a string.*

'To lead' (verb) means 'to guide', 'to direct', etc. It also rhymes with 'need':
The experienced climber had to lead the others.

The past tense of 'lead' is 'led', and this word also rhymes with 'fed'. Can you see now where the confusion arises? It's a pronunciation problem between the noun 'lead' and the past tense of 'lead', which is 'led'.

The assistance dog led his owner across the road. ✔
Not: *The assistance dog lead his owner across the road.* ✘

I hope this sorts this out for you once and for all. To check, you may find it helps to read aloud any sentence containing one of these words.

TIP 176
Lets or Let's

Just another example of careless, thoughtless writing. This mistake usually happens when the first (*lets*) is written instead of the second (*let's*).

'Lets' is the third person (he, she, it) of the verb meaning 'to allow' or 'to hire out':
His mother lets him stay up late. The property owner lets out his six houses.
'Let's' is the one you're likely to use more. This is an abbreviation of 'let us':
Let's go for a walk.

TIP 177 Libel or Slander (Advanced Point)
Both are statements likely to damage someone's good reputation. **Libel is written; slander is spoken** (to remember the difference, think of 's' and 's' in slander/spoken):
What she wrote about her rival amounted to libel.
What she said about her rival amounted to slander.

TIP 178 Like or As (If) and Such As (Advanced Point)
'Like' is a preposition and is always followed by a noun, pronoun or a few words to make a prepositional phrase: *She looks exactly like her mother.*

It shouldn't be used with a clause in Standard English. Use 'as if':
It looks like the man has stolen it. ✘ *It looks as if the man has stolen it.* ✔

'As' is a conjunction, and must be followed by a clause containing a subject and a verb.
'Like' cannot be used here: *She enjoys life, like most girls her age do.* ✘
She enjoys life, as most girls her age do. ✔

Don't substitute 'like' for 'such as' in the following, where there's a suggestion of giving an example: *Languages like Greek and Latin are not widely taught today.* ✘
Languages such as Greek and Latin are not widely taught today. ✔

TIP 179 Loath or Loathe
'Loath' (adjective) **means 'reluctant' or 'disinclined'.** It has the same sound as 'both'. Its feeling is less intense than that of 'loathe': *I was loath to touch it!*
'Loathe' (verb) **means 'to regard with disgust' or 'detest'.** Its final 'th' sound is the same as that in 'breathe': *Bernard loathes snakes.*

TIP 180
Loose or Lose
This is an *extremely* common error, one of the worst! **It usually happens when 'loose' is used for 'lose'.**

I once read on a website whose webmaster certainly should have known better:
"Don't loose £800 – apply today."

'Loose' (adjective) **means 'not tight' and rhymes with 'juice':**
My teeth were loose. The window was loose.
'Lose' (verb) **means 'to cease to have' and rhymes with 'choose'.** It often gives problems in the gerund: *Be careful not to lose your money.* ✔ *Not many people like loosing (gerund) at cards.* ✘ *Not many people like losing at cards.* ✔

Read all these examples aloud, and, again, *think* next time you want to write one of them.

TIP 181
May or Might
One of the worst mistakes in the English language is the use of 'may' for 'might'.

'May' is a stronger form of 'might', when used for probability. This is quite straightforward: *We may go to Venice next year.*

I'm sure you can understand that this is a more likely probability than:
We might go to Venice next year.

'May' seems to have completely obliterated 'might' in the speech and writing of many people. Let's try to work out why they're wrong to make this substitution.

'May' refers to a probability which could happen in the *future*:
She may graduate next year. They may make a success of their business.

It's impossible to know if such events will come about because they have *not yet happened*.

'Might' is the past tense of 'may': *She might* (not 'may') *have graduated, but she failed to do so. They might* (not 'may') *have made a success of their business, but unfortunately they selected the wrong product.*

Look at these again. The 'may' examples refer to an uncertain *future*, whereas the 'might' examples tell of a possibility or probability in the *past* that certainly did *not* happen.

If you hear a first clause in the past tense, you should notice that 'might' rather than 'may' will be required: *The man got up* (past tense) *early so that he might* (not 'may') *catch the train. Had she been tried* (past tense) *today and not 40 years ago, she might* (not 'may') *not have been imprisoned.*

Sometimes either will do, with a slight difference in the meaning:
He may be coming.
He might be coming.
Which one implies he is more likely to be coming?

TIP 182 Maybe or May Be
It may be that you confuse 'may be' and 'maybe'.
'Maybe' is another word for 'perhaps' or 'possibly':
Maybe everyone will get this right in future.
'May be' is the modal verb 'may' plus 'be':
The current has an undertow, and she fears he may be drowned.

TIP 183 Moral or Morale
'Moral' is an adjective meaning 'concerned with goodness or badness of human character': *"The law is not a moral profession."* [Queen Victoria]
'Morale' is what is raised or lowered according to circumstances:
Her morale went up considerably when she discovered that she had won first prize.

TIP 184 No one or No-one
The answer is 'no one'. *'No-one'* doesn't exist.

TIP 185 Onto or On To
He jumped down from the wall onto the beach. ✔
He journeyed on to the next island. ✔

In the first example, there is a preposition 'onto' plus a noun, 'beach'; whereas in the second example 'on' (adverb) is connected to the verb 'journeyed'.

TIP 186 Overlook or Oversee

'Overlook' means to fail to notice, or to condone: *Their cottage overlooked the harbour. John's father could not overlook his shocking behaviour.*
'Oversee' is to officially supervise work or workers:
The inspector visited each day to oversee the construction of the building.

TIP 187 Passed or Past

'Passed' is the past tense of the verb 'to pass': *The train passed Naples on its way to Sicily.* The dog *passed away* (a euphemistic use – see TIP 329).
'Past' (noun) means 'the time before now': *We cannot change our past.*
'Past' (adjective) meaning 'before now': *"Give me back my past years."* [Virgil]

TIP 188 Personal or Personnel

'Personal' is an adjective, meaning 'one's own', 'private':
"Personal relations are the important thing for ever and ever." [E. M. Forster]
'Personnel' (noun) often refers to a 'body of employees'.

TIP 189
Practice or Practise

'Practice' (noun) means 'habitual action': *It's my regular practice to get up at dawn. Practice makes perfect.*
'Practise' (verb) means 'to perform habitually': *Practise what you preach.*
And the words of an impatient actor: *"I wish, sir, you would practise this without me. I can't stay dying here all night."* [Richard Brinsley Sheridan]

As suggested elsewhere, if you need a rule of thumb to remember the difference in spelling between the noun and the verb (the same also applies to 'licence' and 'license'), just think of 'advice' (noun) and 'advise' (verb), where the pronunciation of the two words is different (see TIP 93).

If you come from the United States, disregard all the above, as you use 'practice' for both noun and verb – how sensible!

TIP 190
Principal or Principle

'Principal' (noun, adjective) means 'first in rank or importance', 'chief':
The new principal (noun) was more popular than his predecessor was. The principal (adjective) boy in a pantomime is always a girl!
'Principle' (noun) means a 'fundamental truth', a 'personal code of conduct': *"The one great principle of the English law is to make business for itself."* [Charles Dickens]

Note that confusing these two is *very* common.

TIP 191 Precede or Proceed

'Precede' (to come before): *Writing a book precedes publishing it.*
'Proceed' (to continue): *She proceeded to tell the whole story.*

TIP 192 Prophecy or Prophesy
'Prophecy' (noun) means 'a prediction of future events':
The prophecy of Isaiah is recounted in the Bible.
'Prophesy' (verb) means 'to foretell': *Isaiah prophesied the birth of Jesus.*

TIP 193
Provided or Providing
These two are confused all the time, but only one way round: 'providing' (e.g.
providing you pay on time) is used instead of 'provided'.
'Provided' (often followed by 'that') means 'on the condition or understanding':
Provided (that) you've finished your work, you may go.
You can have it, provided (that) you've got enough money.
'Providing' is the present participle and gerund of the verb 'to provide':
Will you be providing all the food? Providing the music is Lynne's job.

TIP 194 Quiet or Quite
'Quiet' (adjective) is the opposite of noisy:
"Anything for a quiet life." [Thomas Middleton]
'Quite' (adverb) means, among other things, 'to some extent':
By nine o'clock, I'm quite tired.

And a final example with both: *The baby was quite quiet during the wedding ceremony.*

Be careful also with 'dairy' and 'diary', 'tired' and 'tried', where it's easy to make
similar transpositions of letters.

TIP 195 Raise or Rise
'Raise' is a transitive verb (TIP 33):
He raised his hand when he saw a friend on the other side of the street.
'Rise' is an intransitive verb (TIP 34): *She tried to rise, but fell back onto the bed.*

TIP 196 Review or Revue
**'Review' has several meanings, e.g. a general assessment or survey of a person or
thing:** *His play was reviewed by the journalist from the local newspaper.*
A 'revue' is a theatrical entertainment consisting of a number of short items.

TIP 197 Role or Roll
You're not likely, I should imagine, to confuse your bread roll with your role in the
local play.
'Roll' can also be a verb.
"We are the Walt Disney corporation, and we don't roll over for anyone." [Anonymous]

TIP 198
Sat or Sitting
Here are two incorrect examples: *I was sat in my house, reading a book.* ✖
Sat in the train, I could see the sunset. ✖

Let's correct these: *I was sitting in my house, reading a book.* ✔
Sitting in the train, I could see the sunset. ✔

This is a continuous/progressive use of the verb; in other words, the action goes on for some time. These tenses are formed from the present tense ('sleep', 'swim', 'dig', 'lose', etc.) plus –ing: *I was sleeping, you were swimming, he was digging, they were losing.* ✔ *I was sitting.* ✔

Perhaps the error arises because 'I was sat' does exist, but *only if someone else sits you down.* This is a passive construction, such as: *I was hit, you were taught, he was met,* where someone else does the hitting, teaching or meeting.

It may help to think of this construction in terms of smaller people (or animals), when you could say: *The mother picked up the baby and sat him on my lap.*

So, *The baby was sat on my lap*, a quick action done by a third person (the mother), is not the same thing as *The baby was sitting on my lap*, which could go on for some length of time.

Before going on, look at **Stood or Standing** (TIP 205), which works grammatically in the same way.

TIP 199 Shear or Sheer
'Shear' (verb) **is what you do to sheep.**
'Sheer' (adjective) **means 'absolute', 'very steep', etc.:**
There was a sheer drop at the edge of the road.

TIP 200 Short or Shortly
'Short' (adjective) **means 'not tall', or** (adverb) **'before the expected time':**
The meeting was cut short (adverb) *by a short* (adjective) *speech from the chairman.*
'Shortly' (adverb) **means 'before long, soon':** *The bus will arrive shortly.*

TIP 201 Sight or Site
Apart from their sound, the two have nothing in common:
"a monster horrendous, hideous and vast, deprived of sight." [Virgil]
The site of the new hospital had been chosen.

TIP 202 Sole or Soul
'Sole' (noun) **means 'under-surface of the foot', or is the name of a fish, and, as an adjective, 'one and only':** *The sole of my shoe was loose. I am a sole* (adjective) *trader. The lemon sole was delicious!*
'Soul' (noun) **means 'the spiritual part of a human being':**
"Jesu, lover of my soul..." [Charles Wesley]

TIP 203 Stalactites or Stalagmites
I could never remember the difference until I realised that stalaCtites grow from the Ceiling; whereas stalaGmites grow from the Ground. But I expect you already knew that.

TIP 204
Stationary or Stationery

The mistake is usually to write 'stationary' for 'stationery'.
'Stationary' (adjective) **means 'not moving':** *Her car collided with a stationary van.*
'Stationery' (noun) **is writing materials:** Used as an adjective:
She collided with a stationery van (i.e. one carrying stationery).

I always remember this one by thinking of:
* stAtionAry cAr
* stationEry is EnvElopEs for lEttEers

 TIP 205
Stood or Standing

Apart from the fact that the verb is different, the error is identical with 'sat/sitting', and all the reasons I've given above apply here too.

He was stood at the bus stop. (Not unless someone picked him up and placed him there – unlikely!) ✗ *He was standing at the bus stop.* ✓

You'll know now why… *The child was stood on a chair* (by another person) doesn't mean the same as: *The child was standing on a chair.*

Unfortunately, this error, which stems from taking the wrong part of the verb, is increasing. Listen for: 'I was knelt' instead of 'I was kneeling'; 'it was nestled' instead of 'it was nestling', etc. You know better!

This abomination is creeping inexorably towards being treated as correct.

TIP 206 ~~ht~~ or Strait

These are pronou~~~~d the same, but have different meanings.
'Straight' (adjective) ~~~~eans **'not curved or bent':** *She had straight hair.*
'Strait' (noun) **is a narrow area of sea between two pieces of land:**
The Straits of Gibraltar.

TIP 207 Style or Stile

'Style' is the manner or fashion of doing or wearing something:
"If at first you don't succeed, failure may be your style." [Quentin Crisp]
'Stile' is what you use to cross a fence or hedge.

TIP 208 Testament or Testimony

These are two entirely different nouns, yet the first seems to be the only one used, for both!

'Testament' is a will. Many will know these two words used together:
last will and testament.
'Testimony' is a verification or evidence in support of a fact or statement:
The excellent state of the grounds was testimony to the hard work of the gardeners.

TIP 209 Than or Then
Use 'than' (conjunction) **when you're comparing two or more things or people:**
You're taller than she is.
Use 'then' (adverb) **for 'at that time':** *She cleaned her teeth, and then she went to bed.*

Some people scatter the word 'then' all over the place. Only use it when you need it, as in the example immediately above, to show that one action follows another.

TIP 210
Their, They're or There
You shouldn't confuse these, as they're all very different – apart from their sound. It's this similarity that probably makes people use the wrong one: they just don't think!

'Their' is a possessive adjective meaning 'belonging to them', and it describes a noun: *Their house was always welcoming.*
'They're' is a contraction or abbreviated form of 'they are':
I think they're coming home tomorrow.
'There' indicates position: *The dog was over there, in the corner.*

Now two contrived examples with all three: *They're leaving all their cats there. They're on their way there.*

Be very careful *not* to write: *They collected there money.*

Some people are helped by thinking of the last four letters of 'there' and linking this word of place with 'here' and 'where'. If you apply this 'rule' to the incorrect example in the Note, you'll see why this is wrong.

TIP 211
There Is or There Are
Whether to use 'there is' or 'there are' depends on what comes after 'there'.

'There' is an adverb, and the verb agrees with the subject following the verb 'is' or 'are' (and, of course, similarly other tenses, e.g. 'there was' or 'there were').
'There is' is often shortened in speech to 'there's'.

Look first at the types of mistakes sometimes made: *There's crowds of people outside.* ✗
There was other ideas on how to deal with the problem. ✗

Because the word coming after the verb is plural, the verb must be plural, as in these corrections: *There are crowds of people outside.* ✓

There were other ideas on how to deal with the problem. ✔

The mistake may be made because there is no abbreviated form of 'there are', so 'there's' is used for both singular and plural.

Similarly, 'here is' (here's) and 'here are':
Why is the following example wrong? *Here's your documents.* ✘
Corrected: *Here are your documents.* ✔

TIP 212 There's or Theirs ˋ
'There's' is the contracted form of 'there is': *There's a hole in my bucket…*
'Theirs' is a possessive pronoun: *This car isn't mine; it's theirs.*

TIP 213 This, That, These, Those
These are easy, but are used incorrectly by those who don't think sometimes:
this (sort/kind/type of thing*)
that (sort/kind/type of thing)
these (sorts/kinds/types of things)
those (sorts/kinds/types of things)
* 'thing' could be any noun, e.g. food, work, book, etc.
I do dislike those kind of people. ✘ *I do dislike those kinds of people.* ✔
These sort of games are boring. ✘ *These sorts of games are boring.* ✔

'These' and 'those' are determiners that go with plural nouns, so:
I do dislike those kinds of people. ✔ *These sorts of exercises are exhausting.* ✔

Or, put into the singular: *I do dislike this kind of person.* ✔
This sort of exercise is exhausting. ✔ (My spellchecker knows this one.)

TIP 214 Tide or Tied
"He's going out with the tide." [Charles Dickens]
"I would rather be tied to the soil as another man's serf…" [Homer]

 TIP 215
To, Too or Two
This point is very elementary, but people do make mistakes, even if it's just a typo, with these three:
'To' is the first word of an infinitive, or the first word of a prepositional phrase:
I'm going to Florence (phrase) *to see* (infinitive) *the cathedral.*
'Too' is an adverb meaning 'also' or 'to a great extent':
I'm too tired to do any more work. "And her mother came too!" [Dion Titheradge]

I saw this once: *Get this information before it's to late.*

'Two' is a number, as I know you know: *She drank two cups of coffee.*

Finally, an example with all three:
She was too thirsty to drink fewer than two cups of coffee.

TIP 216 Told or Tolled
'Told' is, of course, the far more common of this pair: *"Sadder than owl-songs or the midnight blast, / Is that portentous phrase, 'I told you so'."* [Lord Byron] (You might like to work out the inverted commas in the Byron example and try to write something similar yourself.)
'Tolled', the past tense of 'toll', is something you do to a bell. You ring bells for happy occasions and toll them for funerals.

TIP 217 Unique
'Unique' means 'one of a kind', so it can't be modified or added to. You can't say something is 'so unique', or 'very unique' or 'rather unique'. Just 'unique':
Every person is unique: no two people are the same. ✓
His way of singing is very unique. ✗ (Remove 'very'.)

If you feel a need to modify 'unique', think of another word which you *can* modify:
His singing is more unique than is hers. ✗
Change to: *His singing is more unusual than is hers.* ✓

Here are a few other words that are complete in themselves:
dead, eternal, final, identical, infinite, mortal, perfect, straight

Try to modify them. In most cases, you can't. But you could, for example, say 'almost identical'.

TIP 218 Waist or Waste
'Waist' (noun) **is the area between your ribs and the lower part of your body:**
She has a very narrow waist.
'Waste' (noun, adjective or verb) **means 'useless remains' or 'fail to use':**
Don't waste water.
I was somewhat surprised to read one day: *Let's not waist any more time.* ✗

TIP 219 Waive or Wave
'Waive' means 'refrain from insisting upon': *The fine was waived.*
You'll know 'wave' (here used as a noun; but it can also be a verb):
"We sat on the front and watched the hardy English children... advancing, mauve with cold, into the cheerless waves." [Noël Coward]

TIP 220 Wander or Wonder
Two verbs with very different meanings, but only one letter different, so take care.

'Wander' means to 'go about from place to place aimlessly':
"[I] love to wander in that golden maze." [John Dryden]

'Wonder' is 'to be curious to know': *She wondered if there was a lake in the park.*

TIP 221 Weather or Whether

Again, if you confuse these, it's probably a slip – but I've seen 'weather' used for 'whether', perhaps because the first word was learned at a younger age?

'Weather' is what many people talk about much of the time:
What's the weather like in San Diego at the moment?
'Whether' (conjunction) **introduces one or more alternative possibilities.** It can often be replaced by 'if': *I wonder whether they will come. I wonder if they will come.*

Now both: *I wondered whether the weather would be fine for the football match.*

TIP 222 Were or Where

'Were' is part of the past tense of the verb 'to be':
We were looking for a black car, not a blue one.
'Where' is a question word: *Where are my trainers?*

Now both: *Where were you last night?*

TIP 223 Who or Whom

'Who' is a subject pronoun: *Who is the best dressed?*
'Whom' is an object pronoun: *I saw three men, one of whom was wearing a red sweater.*

'Whom' has largely disappeared, though purists continue to use it. It's still used quite frequently after a preposition, such as 'by', 'with', 'from', 'for':
To whom it may concern. This is the man from whom the parcel was stolen.

 TIP 224
Whose or Who's

Confusing 'whose' and 'who's' is another very common and thoughtless error. It's made both ways round, depending on which one of the two the writer happens to know or alight on at the time of writing.

'Whose' is the possessive form of 'who' and means 'belonging to whom or which':
Whose is this magazine? The girl whose photograph won the competition was only 15.
'Who's' is a contraction of 'who is' or 'who has'. Note the apostrophe showing the missing letter: *Who's coming to dinner? Who's afraid of the big bad wolf?*

TIP 225 Woman or Women

Don't make the mistake of confusing the spelling of these.
'Woman' is the singular: *"To one of woman born."* [William Shakespeare]
'Women' is the plural:
"Always suspect any job men willingly vacate for women." [Jill Tweedie]

Look at these examples in the possessive form:
This is a woman's group.
These are women's groups.

TIP 226
Your or You're
'Your' is a possessive adjective meaning 'belonging to you': *Is this your coat?*
'You're' is a contraction of 'you are': *You're early!* ✔
You're product is ideal for the market. ✘

I've seen the last one! I'm sure you can correct it.

 The most common error with these is a typo, as in the following example:
Last date for you competition entry is tomorrow. ✘

Unit 2: Review

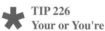

Write the correct option from the two given. Answers on Page 153.

1. The advanced/advance driving test was very difficult.
2. She gave me good advise/advice about my English.
3. The cold weather affected/effected her hands.
4. The speed of her new computer allowed/enabled her to work quicker.
5. The child was not aloud/allowed to go out.
6. There was a lot/alot of interest in the job.
7. Are you all ready/already?
8. The doctor told me that I was alright/all right.
9. All together/Altogether, the work took five hours.
10. I all ways/always say you should try all ways/always.
11. She allocated the jobs between/among all those present.
12. Is it immoral/amoral to lie?
13. He had a large amount/number of books.
14. I'm not going there anymore/any more.
15. Anyone/Any one can do that!
16. You can collect it any time/anytime you like.
17. You can pack the case anyway/any way you like.
18. Our/are books our/are on the table.
19. I assure/ensure/insure my house.
20. Open carefully to avoid/prevent damage.
21. The children behaved bad/badly yesterday.
22. The reason he could not come was because/that he had to work.

23. Between you and I/me, I think she's lazy.
24. I am bored/board with writing questions.
25. Be careful not to brake/break the seal!
26. I couldn't breathe/breath when I ran up the stairs.
27. I decided to by/buy my new shoes at the shop by/buy the church.
28. The castor/caster fell off one of the legs of the old armchair.
29. What stupid childish/childlike behaviour for an adult!
30. The woman had a classic/classical car.
31. Of course/coarse you can come!
32. She compared her answers with/to mine.
33. The man complemented/complimented the singer.
34. It rained continuously/continually on Thursday.
35. The current/currant view is that she was right.
36. The electric fire was defective/deficient.
37. He was dependant/dependent on his wife after his stroke.
38. For desert/dessert she chose chocolate ice cream.
39. She denied that she died/dyed her hair.
40. The parcel was sent direct/directly to his office.
41. She was very uninterested/disinterested in my new fishing rod.
42. I was warned that the wild mushrooms were not eatable/edible.
43. It's not economical/economic to drive to work by car.
44. The parade started at 1800 hours, e.g./i.e. 6 p.m.
45. There were many new language classes, i.e./e.g. Greek and Danish.
46. I tried to elicit/illicit more information from him.
47. She could not get over the enormity/magnitude of the theft.
48. There was a pen, a pencil, a notebook, etc./ect.
49. Every day/Everyday, I see mistakes.
50. I looked for a glass, but every one/everyone was broken.
51. There are fewer/less calories in potatoes than in chips.
52. The journey seemed to go on for ever/forever.
53. Formerly/formally she had been a teacher.
54. The invasion of Iraq was a historical/historic moment.
55. She gave John and I/me lots of information about her childhood.
56. The look on her face inferred/implied that I was lying.
57. He instigated/initiated an inquiry into the murder.
58. We went in to/into the museum.
59. It's/Its not enough to read its contents: you have to remember them!
60. I just/only made three mistakes.
61. She asked me to lay/lie down.
62. The path lead/led through a thick wood.
63. Lets/Let's have a party!
64. I sued her for slander/libel when she openly accused me of lying.
65. It was as if/like I had never opened the book.
66. I didn't want to lose/loose my new friend.
67. We may/might not have got a grant if we hadn't raised some money.
68. She maybe/may be coming tomorrow.
69. The moral/morale of the tale is that cheats never prosper.

70. No-one/No one likes Monday mornings!
71. Now on to/onto the sport…
72. I said that I would overlook/oversee her mistake this time.
73. She passed/past her exam with ease.
74. It was my normal practice/practise to get up at six.
75. As a matter of principal/principle, I think we should not go there.
76. He proceeded/preceded to eat the whole packet.
77. Provided/Providing you're back by twelve, you may go.
78. The child was too quite/quiet.
79. He tried in vain to raise/rise the cover.
80. She played the roll/role of Ophelia.
81. We were sat/sitting in front of the television.
82. The sheer/shear beauty of the lake was breathtaking.
83. I could not tolerate the sight/site of him.
84. I don't like sole/soul music.
85. The train was stationery/stationary.
86. I was stood/standing at the bus stop for 20 minutes.
87. They're/There/Their always shouting.
88. There are/There's one hundred examples here.
89. I think ours is better than their's/theirs.
90. Those sort/sorts of terms are unacceptable.
91. She tied/tide the horse up securely.
92. I am to/too/two tired to think any more!
93. She told/tolled me a lie.
94. The fine was waived/waved.
95. I wonder/wander how many you will get right.
96. The visit depends on whether/weather the whether/weather is fine.
97. Where/Were where/were you yesterday?
98. Who's/Whose is this book?
99. The women/woman were all over 70.
100. You're/Your not coming, are you?

Unit 3: Punctuation

"The system or arrangement of marks used to punctuate a written passage"

Concise Oxford Dictionary

TIP 227 Capital letter: punctuation
The first letter of a sentence: *Once upon a time, there were three bears.*
The first letter of direct or quoted speech: *"Shakespeare is so tiring. You never get to sit down unless you are a king."* [Josephine Hull]

TIP 228 Capital letter: some uses
Proper names of people, places or things: *Nelson Mandela, Pablo Picasso, Alaska, Canada, the Bible, the Koran*

Adjectives from proper nouns: *Australian, Elizabethan, Roman*

Titles of important offices or formal titles:
the President, the Prime Minister, the Pope

Important words in compound titles: *ex-President Clinton, Mayor-elect Malcolm*

Family members: *May I stop now, please, Mum? She's hoping to see Uncle Ken.*

Social titles: Abbreviate except Miss and Master.
You can choose whether or not to use a full stop: *Mr, Mr., Mrs, Mrs., Dr, Dr.*

Days of the week and months: *Wednesday, Sunday, February, August*

Titles of books, films, plays, music, paintings, etc.:
Capitalise the important words and use lower case for less important words:
War and Peace, Gone with the Wind, The Two Gentlemen of Verona, Carmen, Mona Lisa

First lines of poetry:
"When you are old and gray and full of sleep
And nodding by the fire, take down this book,
And slowly read, and dream of the soft look
Your eyes had once, and of their shadows deep…" [W. B. Yeats]

Brand names and logos: *Ford*
Lower case: *adidas*
Whole word: MARIE CLAIRE
Middle of a word: *I used to use* WriteAway *as my business name.*

Abbreviations: USA, BBC

TIP 229 Capital letter: when not to use
1. You may well be aware that it's considered impolite to write entirely in capital letters. This is considered to be SHOUTING! Some people write in capital letters because they think their handwriting is illegible. If you do have to write something by hand, don't write entirely in capital letters. Just use capital letters when you really do want to shout: 'I TOLD you that would happen!'

Of course, you could also have used italics in the sentence above:
'I *told* you that would happen!'

Let's see what happens if we write a whole paragraph in capital letters:

IF YOU WRITE A WHOLE PARAGRAPH IN CAPITAL LETTERS, YOUR READER IS LIKELY TO GET IRRITATED BECAUSE OF THE EFFORT OF TRYING TO READ WHAT YOU'RE SAYING. LETTERS HAVE ASCENDERS AND DESCENDERS (THESE ARE PARTS WHICH GO ABOVE AND BELOW THE LINE), AND THE EYE CAN READ THESE MUCH MORE EASILY THAN LETTERS OF THE SAME SIZE. DON'T DO THIS! ✗

Now read the above in a mixture of upper and lower case letters:

If you write a whole paragraph in capital letters, your reader is likely to get irritated because of the effort of trying to read what you're saying. Letters have ascenders and descenders (these are parts that go above and below the line), and the eye can read these much more easily than letters of the same size. Don't do this! ✓

Which was easier and quicker to read – and took up less space?

2. **Don't capitalise the earth, sun and moon** unless they occur in a list or with other heavenly bodies: *The Earth has one moon only.* ✓ *Most people enjoy the sun.* ✓

3. **Don't capitalise the seasons**, unless there's a specific reason for so doing: *winter, one species of raspberries is called Autumn Bliss.*

TIP 230 Full stop .
The order from the weakest punctuation mark to the strongest is:
Comma, Semicolon, Full stop.

The **colon** (TIPs 260-261) has its own specific uses.

TIP 231 Full stop: when to use
1. **A full stop marks the end of a sentence when it's a complete statement.** It indicates that you should make a slight pause before continuing to the next sentence: *This is a sentence. I can continue with another sentence.*

2. Use a full stop for abbreviations when just the first part of the word is given:
approx., approximately, Tues., Tuesday

TIP 232 Full stop: when not to use
1. Use all capitals and no full stops when abbreviations are pronounced letter by letter: IRA, UN

2. Don't use a full stop in acronyms (words made up of the first letters) pronounced as a word: NATO, AIDS

3. Titles of books, plays, music, paintings, advertising headlines etc. don't have a full stop: *Alice in Wonderland*

TIP 233 Full stop (Advanced Points)
1. Use for abbreviations such as the following (where normally each letter stands for a whole word).

You'll see the following in notes, references, bibliographies etc:

a.m.	*ante meridiem*	*before noon*
c.	*circa*	*about*
e.g.	*exempli gratia*	*for example*
et al.	*et alia*	*and others*
et seq.	*et sequens*	*and the following (pages)*
etc.	*et cetera*	*and the rest*
i.e.	*id est*	*that is*
N.B.	*nota bene*	*note well*
op.	*opus*	*work (of music)*
p.m.	*post meridiem*	*after noon*
q.v.	*quod vide*	*which see (look up a cross-reference)*
viz.	*videlicet*	*namely*

Look at how a few of these are used: *Geoffrey Chaucer was born c. 1340. Beethoven's* Fifth Symphony *(op. 67) is one of his best-known works. N.B. If you don't think, you won't get your grammar right!*

2. If a sentence ends with an abbreviation, don't write a second full stop:
They brought their clothes, books, mobile phones, etc.

However, should your sentence end with a question mark or an exclamation mark, you'll need both: *Do you know the meaning of e.g.?*

TIP 234 Question mark   ?
It's used to show you're asking a question. That said, there are those who seem to be blissfully unaware of this fact.

TIP 235 Question mark: when to use
1. Use a question mark at the end of all direct questions, incomplete questions and statements that are intended to be questions: *When? You're sure?*

"My poor fellow, why not carry a watch?" [Herbert Beerbohm Tree, to a man in the street, carrying a grandfather clock]

However, it's all too often left out, probably because the writer isn't thinking and doesn't remember he/she started with a question word. If you start writing with one of the question words, such as 'who', 'where', 'why', 'when', 'how', the chances are you're launching yourself into a question; so, however long your sentence is and however many words there are from the first to the last, don't lose concentration and forget your question mark!

2. A question mark can be used (often in brackets) if you're not sure about something: *Mrs Preston (mother of 16? children) is the oldest resident in Toronto. Geoffrey Chaucer (1340?–1400) was the first great English poet.*

TIP 236 Question mark: when not to use
1. It isn't used when the question is implied, in indirect/reported speech:
I asked him if he wanted some more coffee.

My actual words, *Would you like some more coffee?*, are not used; I am reporting what I asked.

TIP 237 Question mark (Advanced Points)
1. If you put a question mark in brackets at the end of a sentence, you also require a full stop: *The number of plays William Shakespeare wrote was 37(?).*

2. In the unlikely case that you ask a question about a quotation that is a question, you'll need two: *Which poet asked: "And is there honey still for tea?"?*

If the quotation is not a question, use one as follows:
Did Rupert Brooke say: "History repeats itself; historians repeat each other"?

TIP 238 Exclamation mark   !
An exclamation mark very clearly tells the eye that here is something unusual, some kind of emotion or surprise.

Don't use more than one exclamation mark! If you don't believe me, try your spellchecker on this: *I have read that an exclamation mark is hardly ever required!!*

TIP 239 Exclamation mark: when to use
1. An exclamation mark is used instead of a full stop: *Help!*

2. Use for disapproval: *What a disappointing film!*

3. Use for a command or warning: *Shut that door! Watch out!*

4. Use for disgust, contempt or sarcasm: *Ugh! That's a dreadful thing to do! Sesame Street is about your level!*

5. Use to show emotion or pain: *Ouch!*
"How many torments lie in the small circle of a wedding-ring!" [Colley Cibber]

6. Use to show enthusiasm: *I'd love to come!*

7. Use to show regret or desire: *I wish I could swim! Let me do it!*

8. Use to show surprise: *Good gracious, she's not late!*

TIP 240 Exclamation mark (Advanced Point)
You can grade your emotion with punctuation – did you know that?
No, I don't want to go to bed. No, I don't want to go to bed! No! I don't want to go to bed!

Can you see how the change in punctuation makes this statement stronger each time?

Convey irony by using an exclamation mark within brackets:
That hypocrite (!) told me she was on a diet.

While this exclamation mark is strictly not necessary, it gives strength to what you're writing.

TIP 241 Comma   ,
The uses of the comma are possibly more difficult to explain than those of any other punctuation mark (apart from the apostrophe, which also looks like a comma but chooses to hover above rather than sit on the line).

The comma's main function is to divide up sentences to make them more easily understood. Commas are equivalent to short pauses in speech or reading aloud.

If you just remember that its purpose is to give detail to the structure of sentences, especially longer ones, to make their meaning clearer and easier to understand, this will help a great deal.

Before we go on, look at the sentence above reproduced without commas.

If you just remember that its purpose is to give detail to the structure of sentences especially longer ones to make their meaning clearer and easier to understand this will help a great deal. Not as easy to understand, is it?

TIP 242 Comma: question tag
Look at 'Not as easy to understand, is it?' above. This is one of the easiest uses of the comma.

When you add a question tag to the end of a sentence, you must put a comma before it:
The weather's lovely today, isn't it? He isn't coming, is he?

TIP 243 Comma: with a list
1. **Put commas in a list of nouns or adjectives:** *They met in a cold, damp, dark room.*

Note that there isn't a comma after the last adjective or noun.

2. **If you're writing a list of qualifications, separate each with a comma:**
Janet Masefield MB, BS, MRCS, LRCP, FAAEM, DIBEM, MACOEM

TIP 244 Comma: with a name or title
When addressing someone by name or title, surround the name with commas or the appropriate punctuation:
Karen, this special offer is for you!
This special offer, Karen, is for you!
This special offer is for you, Karen!

TIP 245 Comma: in pairs
The comma is used in pairs in the middle of a sentence to divide off parts of the sentence which are not part of the main statement: *I should like to thank you, ladies and gentlemen, for coming here today. There's no point, as far as I can see, in going on with this discussion. It seems, in the light of what you've just said, that we're wrong.*

Two commas, two brackets and two dashes all serve a similar purpose: to mark off extra information in the middle of a sentence:
I went to see my favourite play, Hamlet, *at Stratford.*
I went to see my favourite play (Hamlet) *at Stratford.*
I went to see my favourite play – Hamlet *– at Stratford.*

But do think about which is most suitable in any particular sentence. Here, the first is the best option. Don't ever use both commas and brackets/dashes.

TIP 246 Comma: with adverbs
When you use an adverb such as 'also', 'besides', 'so, 'indeed', 'instead', 'therefore' etc., put a comma before continuing the sentence: *However, they decided not to go. Nevertheless, they had a good meal.*

If you use such adverbs at the end of a sentence, this is what it will look like:
They decided not to go, however. They had a good meal, nevertheless.

If you use such words in the middle of a sentence, they would need to have commas both sides: *They decided, however, not to go. They had, nevertheless, a good meal.*

Good style dictates that such words normally come at the beginning of the sentence.

TIP 247 Comma: phrases
1. **An introductory phrase about the person or thing following it is separated off with a comma:** *To raise money for the charity, Danny...*

2. If you find yourself writing a prepositional phrase of two or more words, it makes the meaning clearer to use a comma, as in:
Of course, the decision had already been taken.

3. Here's an example of phrases in a series, separated by commas:
Past the stream, up the hill, over the fields…

TIP 248 Comma: clauses
1. If you write a compound or complex sentence, use a comma to separate the clauses. Look at these examples: *"If Winter comes, can Spring be far behind?"* [Percy Bysshe Shelley], *When you've finished eating, would you bring in the washing?*

2. The position of the main clause decides the comma. If you put the main clause first, the comma isn't needed: *I can't write 1,000 words an hour however hard I try. However hard I try, I can't write 1,000 words an hour.*

TIP 249 Comma: with 'and' or 'but'
1. Comma before 'and': *On Saturday, I cleaned the house, did the shopping, weeded the garden, packed my suitcase, and then went to bed.*

In AmE, a comma is always put before the last clause (word, phrase) for clarity. In BrE, this can be omitted and the sentence would read thus: *On Saturday, I cleaned the house, did the shopping, weeded the garden, packed my suitcase and then went to bed.*

Your choice!

2. Is a comma always needed before 'and' or 'but'? Just look at the person or thing which is the subject (the person or thing doing the action of the verb) of the first clause and see whether this changes in the second part of the sentence:
She started with TIP 1 and she worked right through to the end in one week.

Clearly, the subject of both verbs is the same, so no comma before 'and'.

But see the difference in these examples: *The road runs through a valley, and the railway line follows the road closely.*
Christopher wanted to go to France but was persuaded by Jenny to go to Italy.
Christopher wanted to go to France, but Jenny wanted to go to Italy.

Note how the subject, Christopher, is the subject of both clauses in the second sentence above, but not in the third.

 TIP 250
Comma: the worst mistake
Here's the worst mistake with commas. Read and learn! *She studied yoga, it was very interesting.* ✗

Tip: if you ever see the word 'it' immediately after a comma, a bell should ring in your head, because it's more than likely to be an example of incorrect punctuation. In this instance, as in most of this type of sentence, use either a semicolon, the conjunction 'and', or a full stop to make two sentences:

She studied yoga; it was very interesting. ✓
She studied yoga, and it was very interesting. ✓
She studied yoga. It was very interesting. ✓

The first option here is often the best. Don't be afraid of semicolons – some people never use them (see TIPs 256-259).

Try this one yourself, punctuating it in three ways:
I enjoy tennis very much, it's my favourite sport.

If I were to write this, my spellchecker would suggest a semicolon.

TIP 251 Comma: to help meaning
Now a few instances of lack of, or misuse, of the comma in some way.

1. Here's an example which shows how the eye reads on, making the meaning unclear unless there's a comma (it's not the best sentence in the world!): *For tea we had bread and butter was on the table.* **Just put in a comma after 'bread', and this makes sense.**

2. Look at some more examples of where the use of a comma – or the lack of one – makes a difference, even if this is only momentary:
With the police pursuing the people shouted loudly. In the valley below the houses appeared very small. **Put in a comma and these will make sense.**

(Incidentally, no one should ever have to read one of your sentences twice in order to understand its meaning.)

3. In some instances, it's not wrong to put in or leave out a comma; it's just that its inclusion or omission changes the meaning entirely:
However much as I should like to, I cannot go.
However, much as I should like to, I cannot go.

4. You may have learned about separating two ways of saying the same thing with commas (called 'nouns in apposition'): *Noah Webster, the American lexicographer, was reputed to have been found by his wife hunting a fox.*
Messiah, Handel's finest oratorio, was composed in 1742.

In the first example, 'Noah Webster' and 'the American lexicographer' are the same person, and the sentence would still make sense if you removed either.
Similarly, with the second – do it yourself!

When two commas are used in this way (and also whenever two brackets or two dashes are used), it's incorrect to leave out the second one.

5. Beware! You may remember that you need a comma after the subject of the verb (and, yes, you *do* in examples such as those in 4 above). This may lead you to think that you need a comma in *every* sentence after the subject of the verb. Oh no! This misconception leads to mistakes such as: *The newly elected President of the United States, visited Poland.* Fine, if it were to read: *The newly elected President of the United States, Ruth Grace, visited Poland.*

This error happens more often when the subject of the sentence is separated from its verb by several words. If in doubt, just ask yourself – can I take out the section between the two commas and still leave a grammatical sentence?

Here's another incorrect example, where the subject of the sentence and its verb are a long way apart:
Those with the most money and the best education, usually live in large houses.

Here, 'those' and 'live' are so far apart, that some people incorrectly might feel it's time they used a comma. Wrong! The whole subject is 'Those with the most money and the best education'.

6. Right, are you feeling intelligent? This one can cause your brain cells to have to work overtime.

Spot the difference between: *They serve tea which I don't like.* And...
They serve tea, which I don't like.

Just in case you should need an explanation, in the first example they serve a particular brand of tea that I dislike; in the second, I clearly don't like tea at all. OK?

7. Putting in a comma can prevent misunderstanding, as in this example:
The gym was full of healthy young women, tall young men and instructors.
The gym was full of healthy young women, tall young men, and instructors.

Without a comma after 'men', in the second example, the instructors could also appear to be tall.

TIP 252 Comma: with present participle
A comma is used before a present participle ('knowing', 'running', 'thinking' etc.):
I walked down the road, knowing that I was already late.

Look at the difference to the meaning the comma makes here:
I saw a man, driving a car. I saw a man driving a car.

In the first example I was driving; in the second, the man was.

TIP 253 Comma: with 'so'
Use a comma before 'so', when this occurs in the middle of a sentence: *I was in a hurry, so I drove fast – too fast!*

TIP 254 Comma: with numbers
A number of more than three digits requires commas after every third digit from right to left: 6,892,555,109; 98,560,358,002

TIP 255 Comma: when not to use
1. House numbers: *8 George Road*

2. Leave the comma out in such cases as: *a fat old man, a famous French actor*

This is an example of when the first adjective has a close relationship to the noun ('man', 'actor'). Also, to put it in here would unnecessarily slow down the flow of words when reading.

3. Finally, remember that too many commas can be distracting; too few can make a piece of writing difficult to read or, even worse, difficult to understand.

TIP 256 Semicolon   ;
The semicolon isn't half a colon. Their roles are very different. You can see how important they are to some people from this quotation: "*He once telephoned a semicolon from Moscow.*" [James Bone, describing a fastidious journalist]

It's stronger than a comma but weaker than a full stop and is often used to prevent a jerky effect when there's more than one short sentence covering the same subject matter.

TIP 257 Semicolon: uses
1. **The semicolon's main purpose is to unite sentences that are closely associated, or that parallel each other in some way:** "*Worth seeing, yes; but not worth going to see.*" [Samuel Johnson on the Giant's Causeway in Ireland]

2. **It's often used as a stronger divider than a comma in a sentence that already has divisions with commas:**
He came out of the house, which was a short distance from the road, and saw the child run out; but, instead of wondering what the child was doing, he continued on his way.
I should like to thank the leader of the expedition, Frank; the captain of the ship, Peter; the guide, Marcus; and, of course, all the members of the crew.

3. **Use semicolons to separate clauses where there is no conjunction:** "*I hate books; they only teach us about something we know nothing about.*" [Jean-Jacques Rousseau]

4. **Use a semicolon when two clauses are joined by a conjunctive adverb or other expression surrounded by commas:**
I get up at six o'clock; moreover, I do this every day.

TIP 258
Semicolon: not comma

Look at this incorrect use of a comma, where a semicolon is required. Note that 'it' in the middle of a sentence is a danger sign:
The glass slipped out of my hand, it broke on the floor. ✘
The glass slipped out of my hand; it broke on the floor. ✔

TIP 259 Semicolon: when not needed

1. A word you don't normally need a semicolon with is 'and'. The semicolon is usually enough on its own:
There was no malice in him; and he always saw the best side of everyone. ✘

Use either 'and' or a semicolon – not both.

TIP 260 Colon: uses

The colon is another punctuation mark which is sometimes misused – or not used at all through lack of knowledge of how it works.

The colon is a punctuation mark whose typical function is to expand in the second half of the sentence what has preceded in the first half. In other words, there is a clear interdependence between the two clauses:
My uncle may have to go into hospital: he has a kidney infection.

A difference between BrE and AmE is that the former doesn't use a capital letter for the clause after the colon: whereas AmE does this. Here I use the BrE custom, as I have yet to be convinced that one can use a capital letter in the middle of a sentence!

2. Colons can do a balancing job:
The first course of the meal was appalling: the second defied description.

3. As you'll probably recall – and may well have used this many times – a colon introduces a list:
Four main kinds of aid are required at once: electricity, water, food and medical supplies.

The words 'the following' normally give you advance warning that a colon is about to appear.
To punctuate correctly, you need to learn the following: commas, semicolons, colons etc.

Often 'the following' will be on one line and the next part on a new line or lines.

Bullet points (TIP 275) or numbers are often used with this, usually with a new line for each item mentioned.

4. A colon can be used to introduce speech or quoted material:
Murphy's Law states: *"Anything that can go wrong will go wrong."*

Note that the colon comes where a comma normally does, i.e. just before opening the quotation marks.

Should you have occasion to quote a passage of some length from a book, newspaper etc., this would normally be introduced by a colon and indented from the margin to make it stand out from the rest of the text.

5. A colon (or it could be a dash) is sometimes used at the end of a sentence to sum up the earlier part of the sentence. This is a useful stylistic device:
All her concentration was directed towards just one thing: the clock.
All her concentration was directed towards just one thing – the clock.

6. In the text of a play or similar, a colon is used, without quotation marks:
OSCAR WILDE: How I wish I had said that!
WHISTLER: You will, Oscar, you will.

TIP 261 Colon: more simple uses
1. Use it to show the speed of something: She skied down the slope in 2:12 (two minutes, 12 seconds).

2. Book references: Isaiah, 13:8 (the book of Isaiah, Chapter 13, verse 8)

3. A warning on a parcel, a building etc.: Danger: Men at Work

4. Use for a subtitle: English Essentials Explained: *How to Master the Basics of English Grammar, Spelling, Punctuation – and so much more!*

TIP 262 Apostrophe   '
This insignificant little mark in the air causes far more problems than any other punctuation mark! It's either used unnecessarily; or left out when it's needed; or put in where it shouldn't be. Advertisers and webmasters (who should know better and are certainly paid enough for each glaring error the public sees!) are among some of the worst offenders. A quick example here before we go on:
Get the best nights sleep of your life… ✗
Get the best night's sleep of your life… ✓

Often, it seems that people scatter apostrophes about the page as the spirit moves them, without rhyme or reason.

That said, it's probably the hardest punctuation mark to get right consistently. But, if you learn this section and *think*, you should be able to get it right every time – or at least most of the time! One of the problems is that it has two entirely different uses:
1. **to show a contraction**
2. **to show possession**

It's vital you sort these two out in your mind and can recognise which is which when you see or need to use them.

TIP 263 Apostrophe: contractions
The apostrophe is used to show a contraction, namely that a letter or letters have been omitted. This is used all the time in speech and increasingly so in writing:
I'm for *I am, wouldn't* for *would not.*
"I s'pect I growed. Don't think nobody ever made me." [Harriet Beecher Stowe]

And there is the kind of contraction where there is no expansion:
Two o'clock, Will-o'-the-wisp

Apostrophes are used with other contractions, such as: *The '90s*

Remember that contractions are fine in speech, but should not be used in formal writing, e.g. business letters.

Contractions with the verb 'to be': *I'm, You're, He's, She's, It's, We're, They're*

Note that 'he's' can mean 'he is' or 'he has', and similarly with 'she's' and 'it's'. In addition, you can use a noun with these contractions informally: *Mary's coming too.*

In some verbs, 'not' can be contracted: *aren't, can't (cannot), couldn't, doesn't, didn't, haven't, hadn't, isn't, shan't (shall not), wasn't, won't (will not), weren't, wouldn't*

Pronouns and nouns with 'will' (contracted) are: *I'll, you'll, he'll, she'll, it'll, we'll, they'll, Jane'll (she'll) give it to me. (Jane will (she will) give it to me.)*

Similarly, pronouns and nouns with the verb 'to be': *I'm, you're, he's, she's, it's, we're, they're, Ned's ('Ned is' or 'Ned has')*

These are only used in conversation or dialogue, not in formal English.

Contractions with the verb 'to have': *I've, you've, he's, Annie's (Annie has), she's, it's, we've, they've*

Note that 'he's' could be 'he has' or 'he is'. Work this out with 'she's' and 'it's'.

This can lead to a very nasty and all too common mistake. If you contract 'would have', 'could have', 'should have' etc., you'll get: *would've, could've, should've*

This leads to sloppy thinking! Please don't make the increasingly common error of using 'of' after many of the modal verbs (TIP 21), e.g. 'could of', 'might of', 'must of', and the examples above. These don't exist, so banish them from your speech and writing! Some people are even 'bored of'!

What is the 'of'? Think about it – it doesn't exist here. What is needed instead is the contracted form of 'have' ('ve').
You should of known that! ✗ *You should've known that!* ✓
In more formal writing, put: *You should have known that!*

After that rather protracted digression, let's continue with the contracted forms of 'would' and 'had' (these are the same): *I'd, you'd, he'd, she'd, we'd, they'd, you'd better hurry (you had better hurry), I'd rather not! (I would rather not!)*

 TIP 264
Apostrophe: possession

1. **Firstly, bear in mind that you can never split up a whole word with an apostrophe.** So something like Charle's or Jame's or Jone's is just plain wrong. This is because there's no such word as 'Charle', 'Jame' or 'Jone'.

2. **Don't feel you must put in an apostrophe just because there's an 's' around somewhere**. The following rules will explain when an 's' does need one – and where. Don't be like the shop which proclaimed to all: *'Alway's ready to serve you.'* (Another example of where a whole word has been split by an apostrophe, as I'm sure you noticed.)

3. **Think about 'parent's', 'parents'' and 'parents'.** A mistake here could give you one when you have two and vice versa.
A parent's job is never easy. (One parent)
The parents' dance was very enjoyable. (Lots of parents)
"Children begin by loving their parents; after a time they judge them; rarely, if ever, do they forgive them." [Oscar Wilde]

In the third example, there's no hint of an apostrophe: it's just a simple plural: two parents.

4. **Let's think now about the apostrophe before the 's' in a singular noun:**
the boy's father, Harry's teeth
Here you're writing about 'the father of the boy' and 'the teeth of Harry'. To write 'the boys father' or 'Harrys teeth' would be wrong – but seen all too often.

5. **The apostrophe to show possession with plural nouns.** Firstly, those ending in 's', the vast majority of plural nouns, have the apostrophe after the 's', a fact which you'll recall, in all probability:
The boys' games (i.e. the games of more than one boy: one boy would be 'the boy's games')
The birds' nests (i.e. the nests of more than one bird: one bird would be 'the bird's nest')

If the word in the plural doesn't end in 's' because singular and plural are not identical (some of the most common are 'men', 'women', 'children', 'people'), the apostrophe is put, as in a singular noun, before the 's':
the men's habits (compare 'the man's habits') ✔
the women's clothes (compare 'the woman's clothes') ✔
the children's toys (compare 'the child's toys') ✔
the people's identities (compare 'the person's identity') ✔
the peoples' identities ✔ (if you're talking about lots of different peoples, e.g. Swedes, French, Danes etc. grouped together)
You've probably got lost on this last one – don't worry, it'll probably never happen!

It has become almost universal to omit the apostrophe in shops and stores. This is deplorable, wrong and a sign of illiteracy in the writer, the store managers and anyone else who has anything to do with such signage! This kind of mistake can only lead to misuse among those who read such blatant errors in places where someone should know better! Of course, some people think they know about the apostrophe and write as in the second example:

mens clothing, womens department, childrens books ✗
mens' clothing, womens' department, childrens' books ✗
men's clothing, women's department, children's books ✓
(Your spellchecker knows where to put the apostrophe, so use it!)

Avoid *headmistress's* or *headmistresses'* and other triple 's' words – until you're very sure of yourself!

Multiple possessives. Use an apostrophe only in the second named:
Brian Moore's and George Mitchell's new play… ✗
Brian Moore and George Mitchell's new play… ✓

With **length of time**. This one may be new to you and may look like a mistake at first glance. Work it out as follows and you won't go wrong:
We're going back in three years' time (the time of, or belonging to, three years). ✓
The hotel was five minutes' walk from the beach (a walk of five minutes). ✓

Look out for this one – and think. Once you get used to recognising it, this will become second nature, and you won't write, as I saw once:
John has three decades experience as a therapist. ✗

TIP 265 Apostrophe: double possessive
You may (or may not!) have wondered what to say or write in situations such as:
She is a friend of Bob's. ✓ *She is a friend of Bob.* ✗

The first one is correct, because if you reversed it, you wouldn't say: *She is Bob friend.* ✗
You'd say: *She is Bob's friend.* ✓

Another way of remembering this is to think what happens with pronouns.

You wouldn't say: *She is a friend of me.* ✗
But: *She is a friend of mine.* ✓

TIP 266 Apostrophe (Advanced Points)
1. **The apostrophe can also be used to talk about a shop:** *I'm going to the butcher's.*

2. **Another use of the apostrophe is when a word that doesn't normally have a plural is used in the plural:** *He writes b's instead of d's. Her 7's look like 1's.*

3. **How to avoid making a mistake such as:** *Martin Richard highly recommends Mark Hills and Brian Borders new product.*

If you have two people needing apostrophes, just put this with the second:
Martin Richard recommends Mark Hill and Brian Border's new product. ✔
Or: *Martin Richard recommends the new product of Mark Hill and Brian Border.* ✔

4. **You can use apostrophes with indefinite pronouns like 'someone', 'anybody', 'nobody' etc.** *Nobody's coming. This is somebody's umbrella.*

The first is a contraction; the second shows possession.

TIP 267 Apostrophe: when not to use
1. **It's now often omitted in brand names, shops and the names of institutions and publications:** *Mothers Pride, Harrods, Publishers Weekly*

2. **Often, it's left out in such cases as:** *1950s and MPs*

3. In the UK, there is something known by those who do know better as the 'greengrocers' apostrophe'. For some reason best known to them, greengrocers etc. write large signs describing their wares, as follows: *Cabbage's* ✗ *Orange's* ✗ *Potatoe's* ✗ *Banana's* ✗ *Tomatoe's* ✗

Of course, I *do* know why they do it – they see an 's' and remember vaguely something taught at school about an apostrophe having to be inserted before an 's', so they put one!

AN APOSTROPHE IS NEVER USED FOR A PLURAL – which is what they are writing here. Please don't do this! My local supermarket's printed invoice is fine on 'potatoes', 'lemons' etc. but, when it comes to 'avocados', in goes the apostrophe.

Some people seem to want to put them in such words as 'pianos'. I think they think it looks wrong, possibly because of a mispronunciation problem. This would explain why I saw 'top marketing guru's' – I suppose 'gurus' must look odd to some.

Anyway, if you're faced with a word ending in a vowel and you need to make it plural, just add an 's' or an 'es'. A plural I noticed recently was 'virus's'! What should it have been?

Another error I have seen was 'beta tester's'. I've also noticed 'your customer's may'; 'visit their website's'. Tut tut! I can't work out the rationale for these. Probably what Dr Johnson, the writer of the first English dictionary, when confronted by a woman pointing out an error he had made, would have put down to "ignorance, madam, pure ignorance".

I enjoyed a helpful sign I saw once: *Egg's can now be found in Aisle 6.* ✗

TIP 268 Quotation marks or inverted commas " "

Single or double? This is a matter of preference or the common usage in your country – but I'll tell you what I usually do. If using direct speech, I often use two; if quoting a word or phrase, one. Here, I have used two mostly, though not exclusively, for quotations from other authors to differentiate these from anything I have written myself.

TIP 269 Quotation marks: when to use

1. **In direct speech, quotation marks enclose words actually spoken:**
She said, 'I need some new shoes.'
She said, 'I need some new shoes!'
She said, 'May I have some new shoes?'

Note the comma before the first word of her speech and the full stop inside the closing quotation marks.

Correct examples with single quotation marks:
She said, 'I need some new shoes.'
She said, 'I need some new shoes!'
She said, 'May I have some new shoes?'

Study these basic patterns first until you're familiar with them and will never make mistakes again!

2. **Look at what happens if the saying verb comes at the end:**
'I need some new shoes,' she said.
'I need some new shoes!' she stated.
'May I have some new shoes?' she asked.

Note how just to write the rather unexciting verb 'said' in the second and third examples would be inappropriate.

3. **Study how to break up a piece of quoted speech with a verb in the middle.** In the first example, the sentence isn't complete and continues into the second half. In the second, there are two separate sentences (exclamations):
'Hurry up,' she said, 'or you'll miss the train!'
'Go away!' he shouted, 'You're frightening the horses!'

4. Now it becomes a bit trickier. **If you're quoting just a few words and they happen to come at the end of the sentence, the closing inverted comma comes before the punctuation needed to finish the sentence.**
They were described as 'the worst kids on the block'.
They were described as 'the worst kids on the block'!
Were they described as 'the worst kids on the block'?

Many people would get this wrong and put into effect what they thought they know about the punctuation coming *inside* the quotation marks. It doesn't always!

**5. Look what happens if the above examples do come inside direct speech – and
two lots of quotation marks adjoin each other.** Try to work out why each punctuation
mark is in the place it is:

"They were described as 'the worst kids on the block'," she said.
"They were described as 'the worst kids on the block'!" she stated.
"Were they described as 'the worst kids on the block'?" she asked.

If you can understand and use the above, you've mastered the most difficult use of
quotation marks!

6. You can use quotation marks for the names of books, films etc. – or, if you prefer,
use italics – or, if it's common in your country, as in AmE, just underline.

'Jane Eyre'	*Jane Eyre*
'The Times'	*The Times*
'Gone with the Wind'	*Gone with the Wind*

Gone with the Wind is preferable to *Gone With The Wind*. Don't capitalise unimportant
words, as is so often done in long headlines on the Internet. This means every word is
given the same 'weight' – and that's wrong.

**7. If you're writing a conversation between two speakers, start a new line for each
new speaker:**
"What's the weather like in New York?" she asked.
"That depends on the time of year," he replied.
"Yes, of course. Is it cold in winter?"
"It quite often snows."

Note that you can leave out the verb of saying when it's obvious. Note, too, that
contractions are used frequently in direct speech. Forgotten contractions? 'You'll' for
'you will'; 'Katharine's for 'Katharine is/has' etc.

TIP 270 Quotation marks: when not to use
1. Don't use quotation marks for reported speech:
She said that she needed some new shoes.
She stated that she needed some new shoes.
She asked if she could have some new shoes.

Here, you're not using her actual words, but her words reported by someone else. Other
verbs used include *say, tell, ask*.

**2. When a word or group of words is quoted from, for example, a book or a
newspaper, use quotation marks round the actual words 'lifted':**
*What Samuel Johnson described as "the triumph of hope over experience" (a remark
made about a man who remarried immediately after the death of a wife with whom he
had been unhappy) is something more people should perhaps consider.*

3. Lastly, quotation marks can be used to indicate that a word is being used mockingly, sarcastically or light-heartedly:
The 'so-called' wonder diet proved to be ineffective.

Use this device sparingly.

TIP 271 Brackets   ( )

1. Brackets enclose a word or group of words introduced either parenthetically (an addition) into a sentence or by way of explanation. It's important not to use too many, as they can be presumed to be an acknowledgement by the writer that something is being inserted as an afterthought and that the writer has been too lazy to think out in advance what s/he wishes to say.

In the example below, you'll note that there's a whole sentence – in this case an exclamation – inside the brackets. So, the rule in this case is just punctuate as you would do a sentence, and then stick a bracket round each end! Voilà!

When I was a teacher, I was fortunate enough not to have my classes inspected very often. (This was a relief!)

If we just change this slightly, and make it part of the previous sentence, this is what happens: *When I was a teacher, I was fortunate enough not to have my classes inspected very often (this was a relief!).*

Look at this one: *When you're using brackets within a sentence (as I am here), punctuate around them.*

If I were to write this sentence without the brackets, this is what it would look like: *When you're using brackets within a sentence, punctuate around them.*

With the examples above, the sentences would still make sense if the information within the brackets were omitted.

(N.B. this also applies to two commas and two dashes, which, when removed, should leave a complete grammatical sentence.)

If, as in this example…
When you're using brackets within a sentence (as I am here), punctuate around them.
… you need a comma, put it *after* the bracket and never before. Just take out your brackets, if you're unsure. Punctuate the sentence, and then put the bracketed section back in.

Some more examples for you to study: *Zimbabwe (formerly Rhodesia) is a country in Africa. Because they had to pay first (this was obligatory), they decided not to go.*

There are many more, dotted throughout this book. As you come across them (or go back to them), read them in the knowledge that you now know exactly how and why they work *in situ*. And if you don't, study this section again!

When used with discretion, brackets can add a different tone of voice (a sort of confidential aside between the writer and the reader).

The audience applauded the speaker, and the chairman (who had slept through much of the presentation) gave a long, effusive vote of thanks, with little reference to the subject matter of the speech!

2. **On a much simpler level, brackets may be used to enclose reference figures:**
Rule (3) (a)

3. **They are used with dates:** *Johann Sebastian Bach (1685-1750)*

4. **Brackets are used to enclose optional words:** *There are many (apparent) dangers.* (In this example, the dangers may or may not be only apparent.)

5. **Square brackets are used less often. Their main use is to enclose information supplied, often by an editor rather than the writer of the rest of the text:**
She was eating an extrordinary [sic] *amount of ice cream.*

Here the editor wants to show you that s/he knows the spelling is incorrect, but there's a reason why this has not been corrected. (In case you were wondering, 'sic' means 'thus'.)

Square brackets are used in dictionaries, glossaries etc. to show word origins. You'll have noticed them here for authors. amicable [L. *amicus* friend]

6. **Brackets inside brackets. Use square ones as below.**
(The longest poem by John Milton [1608-1674] is 'Paradise Lost'.)
(We went to the best-known opera [Mozart's The Magic Flute*] at Covent Garden.)*

TIP 272 Dash —
Not to be confused with a hyphen – it's longer. **The main difference between the dash and the hyphen is that the dash separates groups of words, whereas the hyphen links words.**

1. **A single dash often introduces a summary:**
The exhibition presents paintings of Wordsworth, Byron, Keats, Shelley, Coleridge and their contemporaries – some fifty portraits in all.

2. **A single dash indicates a slight pause (a colon could also have been used here):**
We decided to go for a walk on the nearby hills – it was such a beautiful day.

3. A single dash may be used when a sentence is left unfinished or is interrupted, or when the writer needs a short pause before his surprising or humorous conclusion:
"I can tell a woman's age in half a minute – and I do!" [W. S. Gilbert]

4. Two dashes are used to indicate asides, rather like the use of two commas or brackets, but giving a more distinct break:
From the start, I was doubtful about the diagnosis – I was sure the doctor was wrong – and this was borne out by subsequent tests.

5. The dash (like the ellipsis, TIP 274) **should not be used as an all-purpose punctuation mark** because you (well, not you) cannot be bothered – or worse, still, don't know – how to use the correct punctuation.

6. A dash can show a sudden change of thought: *The exhibition presents paintings of Wordsworth and Coleridge – have you ever been to the Lake District?*

TIP 273 Hyphen   -
The hyphen joins: the dash separates.

The omission or careless use of the hyphen can cause confusion – read on!

1. Two-part adjectives, when the second part ends in –ed or –ing:
blue-eyed, broken-hearted, good-looking

2. Phrases used as adjectives: *an out-of-work actor, a buy-to-let apartment*

3. Two-part nouns: *paper-shop, make-up, president-elect*

4. Prefixes including 'all', 'anti', 'co', 'ex', 'multi', 'non', 'pre', 'self', 'ultra', 'well': *all-important, anti-hero, co-ordinate, ex-president, non-starter, pre-eminent, self-indulgent, ultra-careful, well-read*

Many words, however, drop the hyphen: *takeover, wideawake*

An exception is when the first word (adverb) ends in 'ly', e.g. 'badly':
It was a badly written letter.

5. If a preposition or adverb is added to a noun, the compound noun now requires a hyphen: *stand-in, go-between, after-effects*

6. If you write as words the numbers from twenty-one to ninety-nine, they need a hyphen: *thirty-three, eighty-eight*

For numbers over ninety-nine, write:
three hundred and eighty-five, six thousand and twenty-two.
Put a hyphen between the tens and units only.

Use a hyphen when fractions are adjectives and when they're written as words:
two-fifths, seven-eighths
There was a three-quarters majority in favour.

But if the fraction is a noun, write: *Seven eighths of the committee voted for the motion.*

7. Sometimes a hyphen is used to prevent misreading or mispronouncing a word:
pre-emptive, counter-revolution, un-American, co-operation

Also, use one to show the difference between:

coop	*co-op*
resign	*re-sign*
resent	*re-sent*

8. A hyphen is required when a proper noun or adjective is preceded by a prefix:
mid-January, post-Dickensian

9. The hyphen is sometimes used when a word would look odd without it:
re-enact, re-educate, re-form (to differentiate this word from 'reform')

10. The hyphen can help meaning as in: *French-speaking people*

Without it, this could mean French people who can speak.

Think, too, what the meaning would be without the hyphen here:
one hundred-odd people, loud-speaker, a cross-section of the audience

11. The hyphen may be used in handwriting (or occasionally with a computer) to divide a word at the end of a line. Words of one syllable can never be divided.

This division should, whenever possible, be made between syllables with a consonant at the beginning of the word on the second line.

If there are hyphens, divide at that point, and always divide so that there isn't something confusing to the eye:
mother-in-law
mother- (line one) *in-law* (line two) ✔
Just think what it would look like if you divided it after 'moth'!
anyone
an-yone ✗ (I saw this in a very reputable UK newspaper!)
any-one ✔

12. There is no rule about:
web site, web-site or *website* (my preference)
fund raising, fund-raising or *fundraising*

world wide, world-wide or *worldwide*
ice cream, ice-cream or *icecream*

All are acceptable. Choose from your favourite dictionary or make up your own mind. My only advice is that you must stick to the same one throughout any particular piece of writing.

If you're not sure whether or not to insert a hyphen and you can't find the word with one in your dictionary, leave it out.

TIP 274 Ellipsis   ...
A very useful device now, if somewhat overused...

Use three – and always three – full stops, followed by a single space... to show that a group of words has been omitted, say when you quote from a document, book etc.

"Eleanor Rigby picks up the rice... Where do they all come from?" [John Lennon and Paul McCartney]

It can, like the dash (TIP 272) prove to be a very lazy way of punctuation... *the ellipsis is used for more or less any other punctuation mark... it saves the writer thinking which one to use... or perhaps s/he actually has very little idea which one to use anyway.*

I exaggerate, of course, but you may see this kind of thing. Used in moderation, the ellipsis can be a very effective device.

 If you end a sentence with an ellipsis, you need a full stop as well or, as here, an exclamation mark...!

TIP 275 Bullet points   •
You'll have seen these elsewhere in this book, and you'll be familiar with their use. I only want to make a few points...

1. Check that the words at the beginning of each bullet point are the same part of speech. For example, most of the words in this list are nouns, so stick to nouns throughout.

Please make sure you have the following:
• money
• how to act in an emergency
• bank details
• passport

- where to ask for help
- map
- your ID card

It's obvious which two are wrong – you could correct them by writing something like: 'instructions on how to act in an emergency' etc. This mistake happens quite often – look out for it – and don't make it yourself. Think!

2. Look at this:
Make sure that you
- have your passport ready
- have full instructions ready
- have your money ready
- have your bank details ready
- have your map ready
- have your ID ready

If a verb is repeated in every line, put the verb before you start the bullet points. I've rather laboured the point here, but I've seen similar examples. You'll have worked out that it would be much easier on the eye to write:

Make sure that you have ready:
- your passport
- full instructions
- your money
- your bank details
- your map
- your ID

Whether or not you use capital letters for each bullet point or punctuate each one has to be judged by the context.

3. Think carefully before you use any 'fancy' bullet points: do they add to or detract from the message you're trying to convey? Don't use them just because they're there.

Note

- If you're using bullet points in advertising material, ensure that your most important point is put first, as this is the one most likely to be remembered.
- The second most important point should be your last, for the same reason.
- You should limit the number of items in your bulleted list to no more than seven, as it's hard for people to absorb more than this number, so you gain nothing by exceeding that number in any one list.

> • Don't end each bullet point with a full stop, as it's obvious where each point ends. Moreover, this slows the reader down, since we are conditioned to pause slightly at a full stop, and you don't want that, as bulleted lists are meant to speed things up.

As you can see, the above list attempts to follow the rules, with a rather ungainly construction in the last one! I have also used full stops, as the above are complete sentences.

TIP 276 Italics

Italics are used for emphasis and in foreign words: The dog was *so* tired. They decided to change the *status quo*.

You may have occasion to write a whole passage in italics. What then happens if you want to put something in italics?

Simple: you just write it in regular type, a device which has been used quite often in this book: *The dog was* absolutely *exhausted*.

TIP 277 Slash   /

This is a 'slanting line used to mark division of words or lines'. It's also known as a forward slash, the word 'forward' being unnecessary, since backward ones aren't used in this context.

Anyway, let's just call it a slash. Sometimes a space is put before and after the slash, so: *The colour was a kind of purple / blue.*

I don't do this, but there's no rule here, so continue if you like it.

1. **It separates parts of a long date:** *The winter of 2010/2011 was very cold.*

2. **To prevent repetition, the slash is used as 'or' in 'and/or' and at other times:**
You can eat cauliflower and/or broccoli.
The instruments required were violins/violas, cellos and double basses.

3. **In a measurement, you can use a slash for the word 'per':** *The car travelled at 110 miles per hour. The car travelled at 110 miles / hour.*

4. **For lines of poetry when, for some reason, you don't wish to start a new line every time the poem does:** *"Shall I compare thee to a Summer's day? / Thou art more lovely and more temperate: / Rough winds do shake the darling buds of May, / And Summer's lease hath all too short a date…"* [William Shakespeare]

It should show the reader that this is verse, probably set out like this to save space. Don't do this for more than four lines, though.

Just before we leave punctuation, I want to emphasise one last time how much punctuation matters. Without it, words can be impossible to understand properly. Just one example: if a television newsreader is presented with an urgent communication, this can only be read easily if it's punctuated properly. So, if you can read something, you can understand it, and can communicate it. When you look at the last question of the Review for Unit 3, it makes little sense without punctuation. Accurate punctuation can't make a bad sentence good, but poor punctuation can make a good sentence bad!

Note

Unit 3: Review

Answer the questions. Answers on Pages 154-155.

1. Put capital letters where required. *tim and james decided to cross the atlantic in a small boat.*
2. Punctuate: *i decided to study russian french and latin*
3. Punctuate: *we saw romeo and juliet last Wednesday*
4. Write this more politely: DID YOU SEE THE FILM LAST NIGHT?
5. Which is the most important punctuation mark?
6. Why is the question mark sometimes forgotten?
7. When is it legitimately left out?
8. What is the main function of a comma?
9. Punctuate this: *the large parcel michael is for you*
10. Use commas where required: *The work up to now has not been too difficult.*
11. *Also there are two more advantages.* Where should there be a comma?
12. Is there a comma here? *If you can't finish it today do it tomorrow.*
13. *She loved denmark it was her favourite country* Punctuate.
14. *One of the best-loved actors, visited our town.* Is this correct?
15. Insert a comma here, if necessary: *I wanted to get home early so I worked very quickly.*
16. Put commas in this number: 12345678
17. Is a semicolon stronger or weaker than a comma?
18. What is the main purpose of the semicolon?
19. Punctuate this: *summer is hot by contrast winter is cold*
20. What is the main purpose of a colon?
21. Put a colon where required here: *I wanted to buy another car mine was very old.*
22. *I wont do any more.* Insert an apostrophe.

23. *Your too late.* Is this correct?
24. *Theyre not coming.* Correct.
25. *I should of known she would be late.* How does this kind of error happen?
26. Put in an apostrophe: *Someones broken my pen.*
27. *My uncles house was near our's.* Is this right?
28. Is this correct? *bottle's and jar's*
29. *Susie I do very much appreciate your help she said.* Punctuate.
30. Punctuate: *clean your shoes she shouted and brush your teeth*
31. Does this sentence require inverted commas/quotation marks? *She said that she would love to visit Finland.*
32. Insert brackets where appropriate: *If you like and you don't have to, you can go tomorrow.*
33. What's the main difference between a dash and a hyphen?
34. Put in the dash: *We decided to have a picnic it was a hot day.*
35. Where should you put hyphens here: *a three legged dog; an ugly looking building; sixty four?*
36. What is an ellipsis?
37. Why should you use this sparingly?
38. Bullet points are a very useful device. What must you be careful about when using them?
39. Why are italics used?
40. What does a slash do?
41. to 50.   Punctuate the following; there won't always be just one right answer.

    oh yes i know what its like to be frightened i remember once when i was about twelve years old i was left in the house it was near christmas and the weather was cold and damp that didnt matter too much though as we had an open fire with hot coals I had been left in charge of my younger brother david and my sister caroline this wasnt the first time in fact it happened often david and caroline were arguing as usual and david pushed caroline too close to the fire there was a guard but it was loose and caroline knocked it to one side she fell towards the hot flames what was I to do

Unit 4: Spelling Rules, Misspellings, Foreign Words and Phrases, Abbreviations

"Words, words, words."
William Shakespeare

Why is spelling so important? Well, you wouldn't expect your bank manager or mortgage lender not to have a good knowledge of mathematics, would you? In the same way, if you're ever to write anything – and who doesn't? – you should know how to spell the words you're using. In addition, a misspelling could lead to an actual error and to your not getting what you wanted or giving completely the wrong impression about something essential.

Spelling is VITAL. A study of more than one thousand people discovered that spelling mistakes in documents irritate over 80% of employers. I'll ignore the fact that the employers' spelling might not be perfect either!

You may wonder why English spelling appears to be so difficult. Briefly, English adopted most of its alphabet from Latin. It also adopted many words from French, Dutch and the Germanic languages, and some from further afield. As a result of this hotchpotch, English spelling is not straightforward, to say the least! The arrival of printing in the 15th and 16th centuries fixed many spellings. Pronunciation did not stand still, though, so this is one of the main reasons why English is not a language where what you see is what you pronounce. You have to spell at times rather like a medieval monk!

Your life is made no easier by the fact that one letter combined with others can be pronounced in a wide variety of ways. Just try saying the following aloud (depending on your accent, of course!):

Ball	(the 'a' sound rhymes with 'all')
Fame	(the 'a' sound rhymes with 'tame')
Father	(the 'a' sound rhymes with 'rather')
Hat	(the 'a' sound rhymes with 'mat')
Many	(the 'a' sound rhymes with the sound in 'penny')
Message	(the 'a' sound rhymes with the sound in 'fridge')
Waffle	(the 'a' sound rhymes with the sound in 'cough')
Was	(the 'a' sound rhymes with the sound in 'lost')

Basically, we're stuck with what sometimes appear to be very irrational spellings. English is not a phonetic language as are, for example, Polish, Spanish or Finnish.

This section considers some of the most important regular rules in English spelling, plus some exceptions to these rules. I have not given you every example nor do I expect you to remember everything here. That is why you have a dictionary!

Let's look first at a term you need to know, suffix.

TIP 278 Spelling: suffix
Vowel suffixes or endings begin with a vowel (and 'y'):
–able, –ed, –er, –est, –ible, –ing, –y (this sounds like a vowel at the end of a word)

Consonant suffixes:
–ful, –ly, –ment, –ness

TIP 279 RULE 1: words ending in –e
1. Words ending in –e drop the –e before a *vowel* suffix, e.g. –able, –ed, –ing, –ous:

state	stating
use	using
hope	hoping
note	notable

2. Keep the –e if the suffix begins with a consonant:

like	likeness
state	statement

Exceptions:

due	duly
true	truly
argue	argument (this is a word you must learn how to spell correctly)

3. Don't drop the –e if there is another vowel next to it:

agree	agreement

4. If a word ends in a consonant plus –le, remove the –e:

terrible	terribly
horrible	horribly

5. If a word ends in –ge, the 'e' is retained to soften the 'g' sound:

courage	courageous
manage	manageable

6. Some words have two possible forms before –able:

like	lik(e)able
move	mov(e)able

7. The following words drop the 'e' because 'e' and 'i' soften 'c' and 'g':

charge	charging
face	facing

judge	judg(e)ment
acknowledge	acknowleg(e)ment

The choice is yours with the last two.

TIP 280 RULE 2: doubling final consonant

In words of one syllable, with a single vowel followed by a single consonant (e.g. 'fat', 'hot'), double the consonant before adding a vowel or 'y' suffix:

thin	*thinner*	*thinnest*	*thinning*
fat	*fatter*	*fattest*	
step	*stepped*	*stepping*	
hot	*hotter*	*hottest*	
sit	*sitter*	*sitting*	
pot	*potty*		

With a *short* vowel ('a' as in 'bat', 'e' as in 'bet', 'i' as in 'bin', 'o' as in 'dot', 'u' as in 'hut'), the rule above works.

Compare the effect of long and short vowels here:

hopping	*hoping*
mopping	*moping*
pinned	*pined*
planned	*planed*

Here are the original words:

hop	*hope*
mop	*mope*
pin	*pine*
plan	*plane*

These consonants are doubled:

b	*sob*	*sobbing*
d	*mad*	*maddest*
g	*fog*	*foggy*
m	*sum*	*summer*
n	*win*	*winner*
p	*tap*	*tapped*
r	*refer*	*referred*
s	*gas*	*gasses* (but not other words ending in –s)
t	*bat*	*batted*

To add a consonant to a word of one syllable, don't double the consonant before adding the suffix:

cup	*cupful*
hard	*hardship*

The final consonant of a two-syllable word may double, following the rule of one short vowel plus one consonant at the end of the word, as above.

prefer	*preferred*	*preferring*
begin	*beginner*	*beginning*
cancel	*cancelling*	*cancelled*
travel	*travelling*	*traveller*

Stressed and unstressed syllables. Consonants are doubled only when the final syllable is stressed:

re*fer*	re*fer*ring	*refe*rence	*refe*ree
pre*fer*	pre*fer*red	*pref*erence	
up*set*	up*set*ting		

But:

*op*en	*op*ening
*off*er	*off*ering
*vi*sit	*vi*sited

TIP 281 **RULE 3: adding –y**

Words ending in a consonant followed by –y change –y to –i before every suffix except –ing.

fury	*furious*
merry	*merrier*
berry	*berries* (and other plurals ending in a consonant plus –y)
apply	*applies* *applied* (but *applying*)

Change –ie to –y before –ing.

die	*dying*
lie	*lying*

Keep the –y if there is a vowel before the –y.

play	*played*
pray	*praying*

Exceptions:

pay	*paid*
lay	*laid*
say	*said*
day	*daily*
gay	*gaily*

TIP 282 **RULE 4: adding –able or –ible**

Look at the rule: **remove –able and a complete word remains. Remove –ible and an incomplete word remains.** This rule works most of the time; but use your dictionary if in doubt.

The –able ending is used for:
a) Non-Latin words
affordable, manageable, renewable, winnable

Take the –able away and see how a complete word remains.

b) New words being coined constantly (note that no words are being 'invented' with –ible endings): *eatable, watchable*

The –ible words are of Latin origin: *admissible, compatible, credible, defensible, digestible, edible, flexible, gullible, horrible, implausible, inaccessible, incredible, indefensible, inedible, intelligible, invincible, irresistible, irreversible, permissible, plausible, possible, reversible, sensible, suggestible, susceptible, tangible, terrible*
If you take off the –ible, in most cases you won't find a complete word. Try a few. Here's one where a complete word does remain: *digestible, digest*

TIP 283 RULE 5: dis– as a prefix
Whether or not you have a double –s depends on whether the root word (the word before the negative prefix 'dis' is added) begins with –s.

Think of these as a sum: a+b=ab.

appear	*dis+appear*	= *disappear*
appoint	*dis+appoint*	= *disappoint*
illusion	*dis+illusion*	= *disillusion*
possess	*dis+possess*	= *dispossess*
satisfy	*dis+satisfy*	= *dissatisfy*
service	*dis+service*	= *disservice*
similar	*dis+similar*	= *dissimilar*

The last three examples have double –s because the root word begins with 's'.
You won't have any more problems with spelling words beginning with 'dis' provided that you remember this rule.

TIP 284 RULE 6: mis– as a prefix
To make a word negative with the prefix mis–, follow the same rule as dis–:

understand	*mis+understand*	= *misunderstand*
apprehension	*mis+apprehension*	= *misapprehension*
manage	*mis+manage*	= *mismanage*
spell	*mis+spell*	= *misspell*

TIP 285 RULE 7: words ending in o–
Words ending in o– usually add es– in the plural:

buffalo	*buffaloes*
cargo	*cargoes*
domino	*dominoes*
echo	*echoes*
go	*goes*
halo	*haloes*
hero	*heroes*
mosquito	*mosquitoes*
motto	*mottoes*

potato	*potatoes*
tomato	*tomatoes*
tornado	*tornadoes*
veto	*vetoes*
volcano	*volcanoes*

Some exceptions to the rule above, e.g. the following from the Italian, have to be learned as you come across or need them:

piano	*pianos*
contralto	*contraltos*
folio	*folios*
studio	*studios*

Your dictionary should tell you whether to put 's' or 'es'.

TIP 286 RULE 8: 'i' before 'e'

1. **You may have learned the rule: 'i' before 'e' except after 'c'. This usually works – PROVIDED THAT THE WORD RHYMES WITH 'ME'.**

One-syllable words: *brief, thief, fierce, grief, grieve, piece, pierce, shield, thief, wield, yield*

Longer words: *achieve, achievement, mischief, mischievous, believe, handkerchief, relief, relieve, retrieve, diesel*

2. **Here are some examples of the rule after 'c':** *ceiling, conceit, conceive, deceit, deceive, perceive, receipt, receive*

The following words don't rhyme with 'me', so are *not* exceptions to this rule. However, they are important words to know how to spell. My advice is that, if there are any here that *you use regularly*, you just learn them.

Rhyme with 'may': *beige, eight, eighth, neighbour, rein, reign, sleigh, veil, vein, weigh, weight*
Rhyme with 'my': *either, neither, height*
Rhyme with 'bin': *foreign, sovereign*
Rhyme with 'been': *caffeine, counterfeit, protein, seize, seizure, weir, weird*
Rhyme with 'it': *forfeit*
Rhyme with 'met': *leisure*
Rhyme with 'air': *their*

You may think 'friend' should be in this list. No, with this word, think of 'end' and put these three letters last: fri*end*.

Names follow no rule: if you know someone with these names, just learn them!
Deirdre, Keith, Neil, Sheila

TIP 287 RULE 9: words ending in –ise and –ize
When you read this, it all depends if you use BrE or AmE, so let's look at both.

1. Usually these verbs are spelled as below:

BrE	AmE
baptise	*baptize*
computerise	*computerize*
realise	*realize*
memorise	*memorize*

Similar are:

analyse	*analyze*
paralyse	*paralyze*

2. Both BrE and AmE spell these two with –ize:
lionize   *capsize*

3. Both BrE and AmE spell these with –ise:
advertise, advise, comprise, compromise, despise, disguise, exercise, franchise,
improvise, merchandise, revise, supervise, surprise, televise

TIP 288 Common misspellings
Now a list of words, included either because they could be spelled or spelt (both are
correct) incorrectly, or because they may help you to widen your vocabulary. The words
were chosen more or less at random and haven't intrinsically any more merit than the
many thousands of other words in the dictionary.

If you don't like my spelling of a word in a particular way because that's not the way
you spell it in your country, that's fine: spell it as you would normally.

All of us have a vocabulary that we never actually use, but it's good to understand
words when you see or hear them. Your writing can improve only if you enlarge your
vocabulary. Putting some or all of these words into sentences will help you a) to spell
the words, and b) to widen your vocabulary. Give yourself a goal of a certain number a
day, say 20. Don't try to do too many at any one time. The next day, look back at your
sentences to check whether you recall the meanings of the words.

If you're unsure of the plural of a noun, a good dictionary will help.

Here are some hints to improve your spelling:
- List alphabetically in a spelling book, or in a folder on your computer, the words
  that you know you sometimes get wrong.
- Remember, a spellchecker can only find spellings. If you've spelled a word
  correctly but misused it, it won't tell you. However, it may warn you with a
  message such as 'Commonly Confused Words' to make you think.
- You must know enough to override your spellchecker when necessary. This
  will come with experience and knowledge, as you continue to study the English

language and how it works. So don't let your spellchecker rule you; you rule your spellchecker.

- Treat your dictionary as your best friend. It contains far more than just the spelling of the word you're looking for. Do what I did once if you have the time: start reading a dictionary! I don't think I finished it.

- A dictionary can help you to pronounce words too. This will help you to spell them. No doubt you, like the majority of people, have your share of words that you have only seen written, so you pronounce them 'your' way, even if only in your head. Just listen to journalists etc. on television and on the radio. Sometimes they pronounce a word you know in a way you don't. Check with your dictionary to find out which of you is right – it could be you.

- Write the word down many times, as you did in school, if its spelling persistently eludes you.

- There are several dictionaries online: just type 'dictionary' in Google or another search engine.

accelerate, accessible, accidentally, accommodation, achieve, acknowledge, acquaintance, address, advantageous, advertisement, aerosol, aggressive, agoraphobia, amicable, analysis, anxiety, apologise, appalling, applause, appreciate, approximately, aquarium, aqueduct, argument, artificial, astrology, astronomy, atmosphere, auspicious, auxiliary, awkward, banister, barbecue, basically, beginning, behaviour, benefactor, beneficial, biased, binoculars, broccoli, brooch, bruise, building, burglar, business, calendar, category, cemetery, centenary, ceremony, changeable, chaos, characteristic, charismatic, chorus, chronic, colossal, column, commemorate, commission, committee, competition, collapsible, conceited, confectionery, confidence, connoisseur, conscientious, conscious, contemporary, controversy, coolly, copious, copyright, correspondence, corridor, courageous, courteous, criticism, crucial, crystal, curiosity, cynical, deceive, decision, defendant, deferential, definite, deny, descent, description, desperate, destruction, desultory, deteriorate, determined, deterrent, develop, dilapidated, dilatory, dilemma, dining, disappear, disappointed, disastrous, discipline, disconsolate, disguise, disintegrate, dissatisfied, dogmatic, domineering, dormitory, drawer, duly, ecstatic, eczema, eerie, eighth, eloquent, embarrassed, emphasise, encyclopaedia, endeavour, enrol, enterprise, enthusiasm, entrepreneur, environment, epigram, eponymous, erroneous, especially, estuary, exaggerate, excessive, exciting, exertion, exhausted, exhibition, exhilarated, existence, experience, exquisite, extinct, extinguish, extraneous, extraordinary, extravagant, extremely, extrovert, facetious, fallacy, fallible, familiar, fascinate, fatality, fatigue, favourite, feasible, fiery, fifth, flexible, fluorescent, focused, foreign, fortuitous, fortunately, fourth, freight, frightened, frugality, fugitive, fulfil, furtive, futility, gallantry, galloping, gardener, gastronome, gauge, genealogical, genial, genuine, geriatric, gesture, ghastly, goodbye, government, gregarious, grievous, guarantee, guardian, guess, guest, guilty, habitat, halve, harass, heir, hilarity, homeopathy, hubris, humorous, hygiene, hypochondriac, hypocrite, idealist, idiosyncrasy, illegible, illusion, imminent, impartial, impatient, impecunious, impediment, imperative, impervious, impostor, incidentally, incognito, independent, infinite, ingenious, innocuous, insuperable, interrupt, intrepid, irascible, iridescent, ironic, irrational, irrelevant, irresistible, irresponsible, irreversible, itinerary, jaded, jealousy, jeopardy, jettison, jewellery, jollity, jubilation, judgement, justifiable, kaleidoscope, kernel, khaki, kilometre, kiosk, knead, knowledgeable, knuckle, language, laughter, league, lethargy, levity, libel, lightning, literally, livelihood, loneliness, loveable, lullaby, luxurious, machinery, maintenance, manoeuvre, mantelpiece, marquee, marvellous, mediocre, melancholy, messenger, metamorphosis, meteorology, meticulous, miniature, minuscule, miscellaneous, mischievous, miserly, misspell, morose, mortgage, murmur, myriad, mysterious, naive, necessity, niece, ninetieth, nucleus, nuisance, notable, noticeable, notorious, nuisance, oasis, obituary, obligatory, obliterate, oblivious, obscure, obsequious, obsolescent, occasionally, occurred, octogenarian, officious, omnipotent, omnipresent, omnivorous, opportune, paid, parallel, paralyse, paraphernalia, parliament, particularly, pedantic, penultimate, percentage, peremptory, perfunctory, perimeter, periodical, permanent, permissible, persuasive, phenomenon, physically, physician, physique, picnicked, plagiarise, platitude, pleasant, possession, practicable, preceding, precipitous, preferred, prejudice, privilege, proceed, procrastinate, professional, profuse, prognosis, prominent, pronunciation, propaganda, propitious, psychological, publicly, pursue, quaint, qualification, quandary, quarantine, quarrel, quarterly, quay, quest, questionable, questionnaire, queuing, quintessence, quixotic, quorum, quotient, radiator, rapport, receipt, recipe, reciprocal, recognise, recommend, recrimination, refectory, referred, regional, regularly, rehearsal, relevant, rendezvous, repetition, representative, repulsive, requisite, reservoir, resilient, resistance, resourceful, responsibility, restaurateur, resuscitate, reversible, rhythm, ridiculous, salutary, sanatorium, satellite, scenery, sceptic, schedule, scheme, sculpture, secretary, seize, sensitive, separate, severely, shining, shrewd, similarly, sincerely, sinecure, sixth, skilfully, solemn, soliloquy, somersault, soporific, souvenir, spelled, sporadic, stoic, straight, strength, stubborn, subtle, succeed, successful, superfluous, supervisor, surprising, survivor, suspicious, swap, technical, temperamental, temperature, temporarily, theatrical, thoroughly, tournament, traditional, tragedy, trepidation, truly, twelfth, typically, tyrannical, ubiquitous, ulterior, ultimate, ultimatum, unacceptable, unanimous, unconscious, unforgettable, unfortunately, uninitiated, unique, unmistakable, unnatural, unnecessary, unusually, vaccine, vacuum, variety, various, vegetarian, vehement, ventilation, veterinary, vicinity, vicious, vigorous, visible, vitality, vocabulary, voluntary, whereas, whim, wholesome, withhold, woollen, worldwide, wrinkle, yacht, yield, zealous, zenith, zoology

TIP 289 Foreign words
Many foreign words and phrases are used every day in English. Here are some you might need, or might be interested to learn. This list of words omits many that I assume you already know (*sofa, judo, bikini*). With one or two exceptions, the following have also been omitted: musical terms, names of animals and plants, food, religion, legal terms (with a few included); and those which required a long explanation.

The list contains some words whose plurals may confuse, plus some which don't have plurals that are commonly used. Sometimes the foreign plural is kept; sometimes the plural is anglicised; sometimes there are both. The different plurals occasionally imply different meanings. If the meaning changes, this is noted. Some words are better known and used sometimes in the singular and sometimes in the plural (*data, minutiae, aquarium, charisma*). Some words have more than one meaning: where space allows, there are two. However, some have several meanings.

The words and phrases are a personal choice because of space (there are literally thousands of foreign words and phrases used in English). If you want to know more, find a book with a title such as *A Dictionary of Foreign Words and Phrases*. A book such as this or a good dictionary will assist with pronunciation if required.

You'll note certain patterns in these plurals, dependent on the word's original language. These are the abbreviations used:

C	Chinese	I	Italian
F	French	J	Japanese
Ge	German	L	Latin
Gr	Greek	Sp	Spanish
He	Hebrew	Sw	Swahili
Hi	Hindi		

Singular	Foreign and English plurals	Meaning
Addendum L	Addenda	Thing to be added
Adieu F	Adieux, Adieus	Goodbye
Agenda L	Agendas	Things to be done; items to be discussed at a meeting
Alibi L	Alibis	Plea that a person was elsewhere at time of event
Alumnus L	Alumni	Former student of a particular place of education
Analysis Gr	Analyses	Detailed examination of item
Antenna L	1. Antennae 2. Antennas	1. Part of an insect 2. Television aerials
Appendix L	1. Appendices 2. Appendixes	1. Part of body 2. Extra sections in books, documents
Aquarium L	Aquaria, Aquariums	Place for fish
Arboretum L	Arboreta, Arboretums	Botanical garden with (rare) trees
Aura L	Aurae, auras	Distinctive atmosphere
Automaton Gr	Automata, Automatons	Mechanism with concealed powers of movement
Axis L	Axes	Fixed imaginary line
Bacterium L	Bacteria	Organisms which may cause disease

Bistro F	Bistros	Small bar or restaurant
Bona fide L	Bona fides (rare, noun)	In good faith/good faith
Bureau F	Bureaux, Bureaus	Writing table with drawers, an office
Charisma Gr	Charismata	Personal magnetism or charm
Château F	Châteaux	Castle or country house
Cherub He	Cherubim, Cherubs	Angel, innocent child
Cognoscente I	Cognoscenti	One who knows, connoisseur
Compendium L	Compendia, Compendiums	One-volume book
Consortium L	Consortia, Consortiums	Association of companies
Crisis Gr	Crises	A decisive moment; time of danger
Criterion Gr	Criteria	Principle something is judged by. Don't use the plural all the time!
Curriculum L	Curricula	Fixed course of study or activities
Curriculum Vitae L	Curricula Vitae	/résumé (AmE)
Datum L	Data (also used for singular)	Facts from which things may be deduced
Diagnosis Gr	Diagnoses	Identification of disease by symptoms
Ditto L	Dittos	The same thing
Emporium Gr	Emporia, Emporiums	Large store with variety of goods
Equilibrium L	Equilibrium, Equilibriums	State of physical balance
Erratum L	Errata	Mistake in printing or writing
Fauna L	Faunae, Faunas	Animals of a region or time
Fiasco I	Fiascos	Complete and humiliating failure
Flora L	Florae, Floras	Plants of a region, time
Formula L	1. Formulae 2. Formulas	1. In mathematical context 2. A set of symbols, words etc.
Forum L	Forums	Assembly place for discussion
Fungus Gr	Fungi, Funguses	Moulds, yeasts, mushrooms etc.
Gateau F	Gateaux, Gâteaux	Cake, usually rich, with cream or fruit
Genius L	Genii, Geniuses	Extraordinarily intelligent person
Graffito I	Graffiti	Drawing or writing on walls etc.
Guru Hi	Gurus	Spiritual teacher or guide, now 'highjacked' by internet experts

Hypothesis Gr	Hypotheses	Proposition as basis for reasoning
Impetus L	Impetuses	Impulse, driving force
Index L	1. Indices 2. Indexes	1. Mathematical, technical, economic uses 2. Lists of references in books
Innuendo L	Innuendos, Innuendoes	An indirect or allusive remark or hint
Kibbutz He	Kibbutzim	Communal agricultural settlement in Israel
Lacuna L	Lacunae, Lacunas	Gap in knowledge
Larva L	Larvae	Insect between egg and pupa
Libretto I	Libretti/Librettos	Text of an opera etc.
Lido I	Lidos	Outdoor swimming pool or beach
Matrix L	Matrices, Matrixes	Interconnected circuit elements
Medium L	Media, Mediums	Mass communication
Memento I	Mementos, Mementoes	Souvenir
Memorandum L	Memoranda, Memorandums	Note to help memory
Milieu F	Milieux, Milieus	Environment or social surroundings
Millennium L	Millennia, Millenniums	Period of 1,000 years
Minutia L	Minutiae	Minor or trivial details
Momentum L	Momenta	Impetus gained by movement
Moratorium L	Moratoria, Moratoriums	Temporary delay
Nucleus L	Nuclei	Central part of cell etc.
Ovum L	Ova	Female egg produced in ovary
Paparazzo I	Paparazzi	Freelance photographer
Parenthesis Gr	Parentheses	An afterthought inserted in a sentence, brackets
Patois F	Patois	Language of a region
Peccadillo Sp	Peccadillos, Peccadilloes	Minor sin, trifling offence
Phenomenon Gr	Phenomena	Remarkable person or thing
Placebo L	Placebos	Medicine containing no drug
Plateau F	Plateaux, Plateaus	High plain
Podium Gr	Podia, Podiums	Small raised platform
Portfolio I	Portfolios	Container for papers, art etc.
Précis F	Précis	Summary
Proscenium L	Proscenia, Prosceniums	Part of stage between curtain and orchestra

Prospectus L	Prospectuses	Information on place, course etc.
Proviso L	Provisos	Condition, stipulation
Putto I	Putti	Cherub in Italian art
Quantum L	Quanta	The smallest possible size
Quorum L	Quorums	Minimum number required to be present
Quota L	Quotas	Share or contribution in proportion
Radius L	Radii, Radiuses	Line from centre to circumference of circle
Referendum L	Referenda, Referendums	Vote taken by electorate on a topic
Replica I	Replicas	Exact copy
Résumé F	Résumés	Summary, curriculum vitae
Rodeo Sp	Rodeos	Rounding up of cattle
Rota L	Rotas	List of names, duties
Safari Sw	Safaris	Trip to see animals in natural habitat
Sanctum L	Sanctums	Holy or private place
Sari Hi	Saris	Traditional Indian dress for women
Scintilla L	Scintillas	A trace, hint of something
Seraph He	Seraphim	An angelic being
Siesta Sp	Siestas	Short midday sleep
Solidus L	Solidi	Oblique stroke, forward slash
Spectrum L	Spectra	Complete range of colours etc.
Stadium L	Stadia, Stadiums	Sports arena
Stigma L	Stigmata, Stigmas	Mark of discredit
Stiletto I	Stilettos	Dagger, shoe with long thin heel
Stimulus L	Stimuli	Something which makes one act
Stratum L	Strata	Horizontal layer of rock etc.
Supremo Sp	Supremos	Supreme head or leader
Syllabus L	Syllabi, Syllabuses	Programme or course of study
Synopsis Gr	Synopses	Summary or outline
Tableau F	Tableaux	Presentation like a picture
Tempo I	Tempi, Tempos	Speed at which music is played
Terminus L	Termini, Terminuses	Where bus/train route ends

Trivium L	Trivia (only used in plural)	Trivialities
Trousseau F	Trousseaux, Trousseaus	Clothes collected for bride for marriage
Tumulus L	Tumuli	Mound of earth
Ultimatum L	Ultimata, Ultimatums	Final statement of conditions
Vertebra L	Vertebrae	Each segment of backbone
Veto L	Vetoes	Refusal to agree
Virago L	Viragos	Bad-tempered, fierce woman
Virtuoso I	Virtuosi, Virtuosos	Skilled performer
Vortex L	Vortices, Vortexes	Whirlpool, whirlwind
Wunderkind Ge	Wunderkinder, Wunderkinds	Child prodigy
Zucchini I	Zucchini	Courgette

TIP 290 Foreign phrases

Linguists may notice that, in places, I've given the more usual meaning rather than a literal translation.

A la carte F	With each dish priced separately
A point F	Cooked exactly right
A priori L	From the cause to the effect
A votre santé! F	Good health, cheers!
Ad hoc L	For a particular purpose
Ad infinitum L	Without end
Ad lib L	At pleasure
Ad nauseam L	To the point of producing nausea
Aide-mémoire F	An aid to memory
Al dente I	Firm when bitten
Alma mater L	Educational establishment attended
Alter ego L	Second self
Amour propre F	Self-esteem
Appellation contrôlée F	Product conforms to strict regulation of quality etc.
Après-ski F	The evening time after skiing
Ars gratia artis L	Art for art's sake

Au contraire F	On the contrary
Au fait F	Having up-to-date knowledge
Au gratin F	With cheese
Au pair F	A foreigner who performs domestic duties for board
Au revoir F	Goodbye
Autre temps, autre moeurs F	Other times, other customs
Avant-garde F	In advance of contemporary taste or trends
Ave atque vale L	Hello and goodbye
Bête noire F	Pet (particular) aversion/dislike
Billet-doux F	A love letter
Bon appétit F	Enjoy your meal
Bon viveur F	Good liver
Bon voyage F	Have a good journey
Bona fide L	In good faith, genuine
Bric-à-brac F	Fancy ware, curiosities
Bureau de change F	Office for exchanging currencies
C'est la vie F	That's life
Ça ne fait rien F	It doesn't matter
Cappuccino I	Frothy coffee with milk
Carpe diem L	Make the most of the present
Carte blanche F	Unlimited power to act
Cause célèbre F	Famous or notorious lawsuit or controversy
Caveat emptor L	Let the buyer beware
Che sarà sarà I	What will be, will be
Chef d'oeuvre F	Masterpiece
Chez nous F	At our house
Cogito ergo sum L	I think, therefore I am
Comme ci comme ça F	Middling, indifferent
Comme il faut F	As it should be
Compos mentis L	In one's right mind
Così così I	So-so, not too bad
Coup d'état F	Sudden overthrow of a government
Coup de foudre F	Love at first sight, sudden, overwhelming event
Crème de la crème F	The best

Cri de coeur F	A heartfelt appeal or protest
Cui bono? L	For whose benefit?
Curriculum vitae L	Outline of education, jobs etc. (résumé AmE)
De facto L	In fact
De jure L	By right, by law
De luxe F	Luxurious, of superior quality
De trop F	Too many, superfluous
Delirium tremens L	Trembling/hallucinations from acute alcoholism
Dolce vita I	A life of luxury and extravagance
Double entendre F	Word or phrase with two meanings
Dramatis personae L	List of characters in a play
Dum spiro spero L	Where there's life there's hope
Embarras de choix F	A confusing number of things to choose from
En bloc F	All together
En famille F	With one's family
En masse F	In a group
En passant F	By the way
En route F	On the way, on the road
En suite F	Forming a unit with
Entre nous F	Between you and me
Esprit de corps F	Spirit of comradeship, loyalty
Ex gratia L	(Payment) as an act of favour
Ex officio L	By virtue of one's office
Fait accompli F	An accomplished fact
Faites vos jeux F	Place your bets (roulette)
Faute de mieux F	For lack of anything better
Faux pas F	A slip or mistake
Feng shui C	Good and bad influences in the environment
Festina lente L	Hurry slowly
Folie de grandeur F	Delusions of grandeur
Force majeure F	Superior power, circumstances outside one's control
Hara kiri J	Method of suicide by disembowelling
Hasta la vista Sp	See you soon
Haute couture F	Designer fashion of very high standard

Hoi polloi Gr	The people, the masses (not 'the' hoi polloi)
Homo sapiens L	Man as a species
Hors de combat F	Out of battle, out of the running
Ici on parle français F	French spoken here
Idée fixe F	Fixed idea, obsession
In camera L	In private
In extremis L	In desperate circumstances
In loco parentis L	In the place of a parent
In situ L	In its place
In vino veritas L	The truth when alcohol has been consumed
Infra dig(nitatem) L	Beneath one's dignity
Inter alia L	Among other things
Ipso facto L	By that very fact
Je ne sais quoi F	An indefinable something
Joie de vivre F	Joy of living
Laissez-faire F	Principle of non-interference
Liberté, egalité, fraternité F	Liberty, equality, fraternity
Lingua franca L	Language common to both/all parties
Magna cum laude L	With great distinction
Magnum opus L	An author's principal work
Maître d'hôtel F	Head waiter, manager
Mal de mer F	Seasickness
Mamma mia I	Exclamation of surprise, wonder, fear, etc. ('My mother')
Man spricht Deutsch Ge	German spoken
Mea culpa L	My fault
Mens sana in corpore sano L	A healthy mind in a healthy body
Mirabile dictu L	Wonderful to relate
Modus operandi L	Way of working
Modus vivendi L	Way of life
Mot juste F	The appropriate word
Nil desperandum L	Don't despair
Noblesse oblige F	Nobility obliges
Nom de plume F	Pen name
Non compos mentis L	Not in one's right mind

Non sequitur L	Something which doesn't follow
Nouveau riche F	New rich
Numero uno I Sp	Most important person
Objet d'art F	Small decorative object
Omnia vincit amor L	Love conquers all
Par avion F	By airmail
Par excellence F	Above all the rest
Pas de deux F	A dance for two people (ballet)
Pas devant les enfants F	Not in front of the children
Per annum L	Each year
Per capita L	For each person
Per se L	In itself
Persona non grata L	An unacceptable person
Pièce de résistance F	Outstanding item
Pied-à-terre F	Dwelling for occasional use
Post mortem L	After-death examination
Pour encourager les autres F	To encourage the others
Premier cru F	Wine of the best quality
Prêt-à-porter F	Ready-to-wear clothes
Primus inter pares L	First among equals
Pro bono L	Legal work done without charge
Pro forma L	As a matter of form
Pro patria L	For one's country
Pro rata L	In proportion
Pro tem(pore) L	For the time being
Quel dommage F	What a pity
Qui s'excuse s'accuse F	He who makes excuses admits responsibility
Quid pro quo L	An equivalent
Quien sabé? Sp	Who knows?
Raison d'être F	Reason for existence
Rien ne va plus F	No more bets (casino)
Sal volatile L	Smelling salts
Sang-froid F	Composure in time of danger
Savoir faire F	Knowledge of the right thing to do

Semper fidelis L	Always faithful
Sic gloria transit mundi L	So the glory of the world passes away
Similia similibus curantur L	Like cures like (homeopathy principle)
Sine die L	Without a fixed day
Sine qua non L	Essential requirement
Son et lumière F	Sound and light outdoor entertainment
Sotto voce I	Spoken very quietly
Status quo L	The existing state of affairs
Sub judice L	Under consideration by judge or court
Sui generis L	Of its own kind, unique
Summa cum laude L	With the highest distinction
Tabula rasa L	Clean slate, fresh start
Tant pis tant mieux F	So much the worse, so much the better
Tempora mutantur L	Times change
Tempus fugit L	Time flies
Terra firma L	Dry land
Tête-à-tête F	Intimate conversation
Tour de force F	Outstanding demonstration of skill, strength etc.
Tout de suite F	Immediately
Tout le monde F	Everyone
Trompe l'oeil F	Art etc. giving a deceptive appearance
Ultra vires L	Beyond one's legal obligation or power
Und so weiter Ge	And so on
Vice versa L	The other way round
Vis-à-vis F	In relation to
Viva voce L	An oral examination
Vive la différence F	Long live the difference
Voilà! F	That's it! There you are!
Vox pop(uli) L	The voice of the people
Wie geht's? Ge	How are you?

TIP 291 Abbreviations

Some of these have been used or mentioned elsewhere. Note how nearly all are derived from Latin. You may see some with full stops (R.S.V.P.) or some without (eg, ie). This is a matter of taste and personal choice. Follow the example of those you trust.

a.m. L	ante meridiem	before noon
c. L	circa	about
CV L	curriculum vitae (BrE)	résumé of jobs, education etc.
DV L	deus volente	God willing
e.g. L	exempli gratia	for example
et al. L	et alia	and others
et seq. L	et sequentes	and the following pages etc.
etc. L	et cetera	and the rest, and so on
i.e. L	id est	that is
N.B. L	nota bene	note well
nem. con. L	neminem contradicente	with no one disagreeing
op. cit. L	opere citato	in the work cited
op. L	opus	work (of music)
p.m. L	post meridiem	after noon
P.S. L	post script	after writing
pp L	per procurationem	on behalf of
q.v. L	quod videre	look up a cross reference
QED L	quod erat demonstrandum	that which was to be proved
RIP L	requiescat in pace	may he/she rest in peace
RSVP F	répondez s'il vous plaît	please reply
viz. L	videlicet	namely

Unit 4: Review

Choose the correct word or answer the questions. Answers on Pages 156-157.

1. She was useing/using my towel.
2. The argument/arguement went on for days.
3. She refered/referred to her notes.
4. She was planing/planning to see him that afternoon.
5. Everyone enjoys storeys/stories.
6. He paid/payed the bill.
7. The path was not accessible/accessable.
8. She was responsible/responsable for the fixtures.
9. It suddenly dissapeared/disappeared.
10. The twins were very disimilar/dissimilar in appearance.
11. She mislaid/misslaid the money.

12. She was misold/missold the pension.
13. The mosquitos/mosquitoes were biting!
14. She used to sing solos/soloes in church.
15. I don't beleive/believe you.
16. The goods were seized/siezed.
17. The child was mischievious/mischievous.
18. She gave me some good advice/advise.
19. I enjoy taking exercise/exercize.

Select the correct spelling:
20. accomodation/accommodation
21. broccoli/brocolli
22. calendar/calender
23. definately/definitely
24. embarrassing/embarassing
25. hygiene/hygeine
26. goverment/government
27. immediatly/immediately
28. liaison/liason
29. misspell/mispell
30. occasionally/occasionly
31. particuly/particularly
32. responsibility/responsability
33. secretry/secretary
34. unnecessary/unnessesry
35. What is the plural of 'appendix'?
36. What is the singular of 'bacteria'?
37. What language does 'cappuccino' come from?
38. What is a 'placebo'?
39. What is a 'terminus'?
40. What does 'à la carte' mean?
41. What is a 'bureau de change'?
42. Where would you hear 'faites vos jeux'?
43. Where does a 'maître d'(hôtel)' work?
44. Who might use a 'nom de plume'?
45. What does 'tempus fugit' mean?
46. What does a.m. mean?
47. Does e.g. or i.e. mean 'for example'?
48. What does etc. mean? Do you know
    what it's short for?
49. What does N.B. mean?
50. Where would you see P.S.?

Unit 5: Style, Drafting, Writing and Proofreading

"True ease in writing comes from art, not chance,
As those move easiest who have learned to dance..."
Alexander Pope

What is style? It's nothing more than the way you write or speak, your fingerprint if you like. You can't write or speak without its being in some kind of style. This is just a *way* of writing or speaking. As you'll read later, your style may be formal or informal or something in between – or even a mixture of all three. The style you use may be deliberate or unconscious. There are times when it needs to be the former, and times when it can be the latter.

People reading your work or listening to you may require this to be in a certain style or register. This section will give details. **It's particularly important that you should be aware of the preferences of others on certain occasions, especially at work, where you study, or elsewhere.**

You already have a style: we all have our own, and no two are alike. **The best style is possibly one you don't notice at all.**

Styles of great writers are recognisable, just as is a painting by Rubens or Picasso. Oscar Wilde stated: *"I don't wish to sign my name, though I am afraid everyone will know who the writer is: one's style is one's signature always."*

The occasions when you should use formal language, informal language and slang are covered here.

TIP 292 Acronyms
Using acronyms is usually acceptable, but you should always write the words out in full the first time, putting the abbreviation in brackets:
The United Nations (UN) decided... It has long been the UN's policy to...

Note

While on the subject of shortened words, don't use these in *formal* writing, as they are wrong:

She couldn't speak	*2 hrs ago*	*8 yrs old*

Write:

She could not speak	*two hours ago*	*eight years old*

TIP 293 Ambiguity

'Ambiguity' is a double meaning, either deliberate or accidentally caused by an expression which may be misunderstood: *No Smoking Bungalows Available.*
She saw her daughter fighting her brother through a crack in the door.
DOCTOR (to overweight patient):   *What's the lightest you've ever been?*
PATIENT: *Seven pounds*

Other instances of ambiguity can occur with pronouns:
She told her daughter that she was going to the dentist.

Who? The mother or the daughter?

As noted in TIP 172, the position of 'only', can cause confusion, as can that of the word 'badly': *Only this shop sells gift vouchers for books. This shop only sells gift vouchers for books. And... She wanted to drive very badly.*

If you use ambiguity deliberately, this must be done with care, otherwise you may lose your reader. It can be used for comic effect, of course.

TIP 294 Ampersand

The ampersand (&) can be useful when you're writing informally; but never use this in business letters or any kind of formal writing:
Would you please sign the enclosed & return it to the office. ✘
Would you please sign the enclosed, and return it to the office. ✔

Always write 'and' in full when writing formally.

TIP 295 Apostrophe: names ending in 's' (Advanced Point)

I recently saw: *Do read Chris' new book about the winter night sky.* Had Chris been Christine, I'm sure the writer would have had no problem in writing: *Do read Christine's new book...* So why not Chris's, which is correct?

When I used to teach, I always told my students *never* to give the characters in their writing a name ending in 's' – so no James or Charles, and no surname such as Williams or Jones. Much easier to use a name without an 's' such as John to prevent that particular pitfall, if there is any choice.

Why? Because if an apostrophe is needed, a name ending in 's' could (and often does) spell trouble because of the need for a second 's', as above.

Think of what you say: do you say 'James wife' or 'Jameses wife'? The latter, of course. So, to write this you would need to spell it 'James's'. It's not incorrect to write James' – but I don't like it. If obligatory, think very carefully about where to put the apostrophe – or avoid it by saying something like 'the wife of James' if this doesn't sound stilted and makes sense in context.

Rule of thumb: if you pronounce the 's' when speaking, add it when writing, e.g. *Keats's poetry*.

So how does this affect style?

If ever you have to invent a name for any reason, just follow this advice. It's more than just a point about punctuation.

If you're using a real name, take extra care. You could impress by getting this right – and vice versa!

Note

To expand the above: problems can arise when you need to make plural a name such as Church, Cox, Jones, Williams – and then make it possessive!

First, remember what you do to these as plurals, e.g. 'bushes', 'churches', and apply that knowledge to the above: *Churches, Coxes, Joneses, Williamses.*

Now all you have to do is put the apostrophe at the end and you have: *the Churches' new house, the Coxes' youngest daughter, the Joneses' quickest route home, the Williamses' sister*

TIP 296 Cliché

A cliché is a tired phrase or word that was once exciting and fresh, but is no longer. However, once a cliché catches the public's imagination, it's used over and over again, until it's worn out, like a pair of old trainers. As Oliver Wendle Holmes Jr. said: *"The minute a phrase becomes current, it becomes an apology for not thinking accurately…"*

Many of them are quite acceptable in speech, though. Here's a list of just a few of the worst offenders plus the kind of pet hates many find annoying: *24/7, All-time high, Are you all right there?, At the end of the day, At this moment in time, Ballpark figure, Bear with me, Bombshell, Don't shoot the messenger, Fit for purpose, For free, For my sins, Heads up, Hopefully, It's not rocket science, Left no stone unturned, Level playing field, No problem, Not a happy bunny, On a daily basis, On the cutting edge, Outside the box, Quantum leap, Same old same old, Sea change, Singing from the same hymn sheet, Slowly but surely, The grass is greener…, The moment of truth, The world and his wife, There you go, Tighten your belt, Water off a duck's back, With all due respect*

Here are suggested replacements for a few clichés:
at present, at the present time	*now*
blueprint	*plan, scheme, proposal*
charisma	*presence, inspiration*

"Let's have some new clichés," said Sam Goldwyn in 1969. Well, we have; but we seem to hang on to them for far too long. If you feel tempted to use any of the above or similar, think twice – and then again – to see whether you can come up with something more original or less disliked!

TIP 297 Colon or dash to sum up

A useful stylistic device is to use a **colon or a dash at the end of a sentence to sum up the earlier part of the sentence**: *"Advice to persons about to marry – don't."* [Punch] *All she wanted in the world could be summed up in one word: health.*

Stronger than a comma but weaker than a full stop, the colon may also be used to prevent a jerky effect when there is more than one short sentence covering the same subject matter: *The boy was the best prospect the school team had: he trained hard daily.*

TIP 298 Commas with sentence adverb

When you use a sentence adverb such as 'also', 'furthermore', 'otherwise', 'indeed', 'therefore', a comma is required before continuing the sentence: *Furthermore, she won the prize for the best student of her year.*

If you put such adverbs at the end of a sentence, this is what you see: *She won the prize for the best student of her year, furthermore.*

When you put this type of adverb in the middle of a sentence, you must surround it with commas: *She won, furthermore, the prize for the best student of her year.*

You can probably see which is best from the point of style: the first.

TIP 299 Conjunction at the beginning of a sentence

You may have been told not to begin a sentence with 'and' or 'but' (or other conjunction). Nonsense! Very effective sentences can start with 'and' or 'but'. But don't use this device too often. And remember, beginning a sentence with 'and' can add emphasis: *"And so to bed."* [Samuel Pepys] *But, my dear friend, I thought you already knew.*

All you have to do is to think whether your preposition would be better lengthening the previous sentence; or whether it would have more emphasis by being the first word of the next sentence.

TIP 300 Hopefully

Hopefully (adverb) **means 'full of hope'.** It doesn't mean 'it is to be hoped that'. Only people can be full of hope.

Look at: *Hopefully, the train will arrive on time.* This is nonsense, because a train can't be full of hope. What you can say is: *We hope that the train will arrive on time. We set out for the summit hopefully.* (The implication here is that we set out for the summit hoping that we would reach it, not that we hoped that we would be able to set out for the summit. If confused by now, just think before using 'hopefully'!)

TIP 301 Idiom

An idiom is a group of words whose meaning is not the same as the words used individually. Idioms are often untranslatable, though similar ones may exist in other languages. As this may sound confusing, let's look at some examples:

Once in a blue moon (very occasionally),

To put your foot down (to insist),

To put your foot in it (to make a mistake),

Thumbs up (a sign of approval),

To play by ear (to play an instrument without being able to read music)

Idioms can prove very difficult for people learning English as a Second Language. They can often prove amusing! If this interests you, look for a dictionary of English idioms.

When writing, you're almost bound to use idioms (even if you don't realise this), as they are used in one form or another all the time.

TIP 302 Infinitive: to split or to not split

As this has already been discussed in TIP 39, I'll be brief here. There are those who do split the infinitive; and those who wouldn't dream of so doing. Some know when they're doing it; others do not. To remind you, this means putting an adverb between 'to' and the verb:

I wanted to quickly open my post to see whether the cheque had arrived.

Splitting the infinitive can make your writing sound more natural. So, if you think this is the case (try it both ways), go ahead.

You may do this in speech: *To really get the relationship right, you need to...*

It may not be a good idea to split an infinitive when writing formally, e.g. in a job application form. It just may be that the person receiving your document has a 'thing' about splitting the infinitive, brands you as 'ignorant' and dismisses your application. It's on a little thing like this that choices are sometimes made!

TIP 303 Jargon

Jargon is used by certain groups of people (computer, business, scientists etc.). They have words that they use to communicate with each other, words that would not normally be known or understood by people outside the profession. Or, the words might have other meanings in the 'real' world. They're used as a kind of shorthand for communication among those who know them. It's considered impolite to use them in front of those who are not familiar with the terminology.

Never use jargon unless there is a specific reason.

Here are some examples from the computer world:

icon, browser, forum, folder

TIP 304 Numbers: how to write

When writing formally, write the numbers one to nine or ten (inclusive) as words:
"There was merely one man fewer." [Prince Mettternich]
"Seven years would be insufficient to make some people acquainted with each other, and seven days are more than enough for others." [Jane Austen]

Words over ten may be (but don't have to be) written as numbers: *I sent 100 Christmas cards last year. I sent one hundred Christmas cards last year. "Nobody loves a fairy when she's forty."* [Arthur W. D. Henley]

When one number is under ten and one over, write both as words:
There were six cakes and fourteen sandwiches left.

Write a number as a word (or words) when this is the first word of a sentence:
Three thousand people attended the rally.
"Thirty-five is a very attractive age. London society is full of women of the very highest birth who have, of their own free choice, remained thirty-five for years." [Oscar Wilde]

TIP 305 Paraphrase or summary

A paraphrase is rewriting in your own words, as freely as you wish – and as long as or even longer than the original – a particular piece of writing. It must explain all the difficult words. In style, it's often less subtle or less beautiful than the original.

A summary has more rules attached: this has to be much shorter than the original: you should pick out just the main points. It's often only about a third of the length of the original. You, like me, may remember it as 'précis'.

If ever asked to produce a paraphrase or a summary, check exactly what is required, as not everyone knows the difference.

TIP 306 Person: when not to change

It's poor style to change from one person to another within a document or piece of writing. In other words, if you begin by using 'we' (first person), don't change to, for example, 'they' (third person).
We hope that you will like our new logo. The company say that they have taken advice and it hopes that you will agree that this one has more impact than the old one.

Do you see how the subject, 'we' (first person) has changed to 'the company' (third person)? Then the writer can't decide if the company is plural ('say') or singular ('it hopes'). Rewrite these sentences correctly. You'll find your spellchecker could help here.

Look out for this kind of sloppy writing – and don't do it yourself!

TIP 307 Preposition at the end of a sentence

Prepositions are usually placed before a group of words to form a prepositional phrase: *under the old oak tree, past the church on the left* (two phrases here)

Some sticklers for good style think that prepositions always have to come before a word or group of words. One reason given is that this was a rule based on Latin, which always has a noun or pronoun following a preposition. So, a preposition can't be left alone at the end of the sentence, they argue, as in: *What is the world coming to? Funny stories are not to be laughed at. This bed has not been slept in.*

However, ignore the rule when, as above, it would be ugly, poor style or impossible to put the preposition anywhere else.

Many people don't like ending a written sentence with a preposition. My advice is to write it as you wish, look at it with the preposition in the two possible places and make up your own mind which sounds better in the particular circumstances. The end could well be the better place.

TIP 308 Register: what is this?
Register is the way of speaking and writing, depending on the circumstances in which you're doing either. Let's go from the most informal to the most formal.

TIP 309 Register: very informal language or slang
Very informal language is outside the scope of *English Essentials Explained*.

Slang is the language often spoken between people who are very close and not judgemental about the English spoken within a particular group, e.g. friends; family; children; close colleagues; members of a team. Its vocabulary and dialect (way of speaking) depend entirely on the people concerned. Only those in the 'group' may speak in this particular way.

Slang is rarely written, except perhaps in short notes.

TIP 310 Register: informal language
Most of us use informal language all the time; this is often quite different from written language. To a lesser or greater extent, the way we speak depends on those we are with; and 'rules' are less important. Sometimes you may notice yourself adapting your style of speech to those around you (you may even have a 'telephone voice'!).

If you're perceptive, you may sometimes feel that you need to do this to make an impression. The change could be 'up' to Standard English or 'down' to slang. Friends and family are unlikely to affect you in this way; neither will they normally criticise or correct your English. For this reason, they may not be your best teachers.

TIP 311 Register: colloquial language
Colloquial language has a vocabulary, a syntax and even a pronunciation (e.g. 'she'll' for 'she will') which are appropriate to conversation among people you know, but which aren't suitable for formal contexts or situations.

Over time, some colloquialisms are promoted to Standard English, while others may be demoted to slang.

A point about pronunciation. Aitch or Haitch? BrE dictionaries give aytch as the standard pronunciation for the letter H. However, the pronunciation haytch is also accepted as a legitimate variant. Haytch is a standard pronunciation in Irish English, and its use by younger English speakers is increasing. That does not mean that I like it!

Note: you may prefer Aitch, Haitch, Haych etc.

TIP 312 Register: which style of writing?

Whenever you're writing anything, you mustn't just let the words crash onto the page in any kind of haphazard manner. Depending on your reader, there is an expected level of linguistic competence. In other words, the same style may not be suitable for both your bank manager and an unskilled person. Only you can be the judge of what style each expects, and deliver this accordingly. You must be aware of, or must make yourself aware of, what style is appropriate on what occasion.

TIP 313 Register: Standard English

Standard English is the name of the type of formal English language used (certainly in all formal documents) by educated people who know and apply the rules of English grammar, both in speech and in writing. Many will have a high level of competence and will rarely make a mistake.

Standard English does not include slang words. However, such words may be used for effect, particularly in fiction, i.e. novels, poetry, drama etc. whenever the writer chooses.

Standard English is the kind of English used in formal situations in the workplace, the courts, the government, educational establishments, medicine, science etc. You're bound to come across one or more of these throughout your life, so it's advisable to know how to use Standard English where and when appropriate.

TIP 314 Style: what is it?

"Style," wrote Jonathan Swift, is *"proper words in proper places."* What that means is a clear and straightforward way of writing which is simple, to the point and well ordered.

Daniel Defoe, the author of *Robinson Crusoe*, defined good style as
"that in which a man speaking to five hundred people... should be understood by them all".

The advice of these two (and of many others before and since) is common to all writing, whether this be an email, an article, a law report, a technical book, a business plan, a letter (personal or business), a novel, a short story etc.

TIP 315 Style: clarity

Let's look at the steps you must follow to be clear:
*   **Unless your *thoughts* are clear, your writing will be as muddled as your**

thoughts. So think first, write second. That's not to say you can't start writing straight away, just that you may need to put order into your random thoughts later on. The computer makes all these revisions so much easier for most people.

- **Get to the point quickly and keep your writing simple.** If you're writing clearly and simply, your grammar should look after itself.
- **Make a list of your main points.** These should not be too many; otherwise you'll overwhelm your reader. A few points made well are worth a hundred made badly.
- **Subdivide your point into sections or headings and put them into a logical order of importance.** Decide which to leave out (this may come later and may keep changing).

TIP 316 Style: which one?

Every piece of work is written in some kind of style. What this is depends on you and, to some extent, on the recipient of your document, be this email, novel, report or whatever.

To illustrate this point, let's look at the style I decided to use for *English Essentials Explained*.

I wanted to make English grammar less daunting and boring than it might have been previously to you, so I've used a light, friendly style. I wanted you to enjoy reading this book and to find it interesting. I imagined I was speaking to you, teaching you and getting across to you my own love for the language and its grammar. I've used the second person, as though you were the only reader of this book.

I use humour, contractions, short tips, lots of space on the page, indeed not too much in any one paragraph, so that you feel you can cope easily with what you're being shown and taught. I do hope I've succeeded!

You'll have noticed that I use both informal and formal English. Every use has been deliberate. Often, far more often than in most books of instruction, I've used contractions. These enable me to 'speak' to you. Having said that, I've written correctly (I trust!) and have used Standard English all the time, except when I've chosen not to.

I'm sure I've made my point: I chose a style and stuck to it. You, too, have to do this with every document you write. This is not as difficult as it sounds. Just imagine you're speaking to a particular person and, knowing that person, be s/he friend or lawyer, you'll naturally adopt the correct style.

Before you begin, ask yourself:
- **Why am I writing?**
- **Whom am I writing for?**
- **Where is this going to be read (home, office etc.)?**

You can't know what style to use unless you can answer these three questions. What, you may ask, if it's for more than one person, situation etc.? In such a case, you'll have to decide if one style is suitable for both or whether some changes may have to be made.

TIP 317 Style: choice of words
You must constantly think about the words you're using.

Your choice of words can induce pleasure, appreciation, sadness, offence and even hatred; so you can see how important it is for you to use the words you intend in every situation.

There are some rules that will help. Use:
* **a shorter rather than a longer word**
* **a familiar rather than an unfamiliar word**
* **a concrete rather than an abstract word**
* **one word rather than several to say the same thing**
* **a simple rather than a complicated word**
* **a word whose spelling you know rather than one you're uncertain about**

TIP 318 Style: vary your words
It's good style to vary your words whenever possible. Whenever you find you're about to write a word you've recently used, think of another similar word whenever possible. If you can't think of one, your thesaurus or your computer's thesaurus will do the job for you.

Rather than writing 'walk' or 'run' more than once, use:
explore, hike, hurry, march, promenade, saunter, stroll, tramp, travel, trek

Do the same exercise with the verb 'to say'. Try to find at least five synonyms (words which mean the same or similar).

TIP 319 Style: lazy words to avoid
Just like clichés, the following words have their place, but usually there's a more stylish word you could choose. Think about this before using them, especially when using Standard English in a formal situation: *a couple of, basically, controversial, fabulous, get, got, in fact, kind of, nice, present, prior to, really, set-up, sort of, you know*

There's often a better word. Let's try this with the verb 'get':

Informal	Formal
I'm getting a new car.	*I'm buying a new car.*
He got fired.	*He lost his job.*
What time will she get there?	*What time will she arrive?*
We've got to go now.	*We must go now.*
They got lots of gifts.	*They received many gifts.*

TIP 320 Style: semicolon
Between a comma and a full stop lies the useful stylistic device called the **semicolon**. Let's consider its main rather neat purpose, **to unite sentences that parallel each other in some way or that are closely associated**: *"When a man is tired of London, he is tired of life; for there is in London all that life can afford."* [Samuel Johnson]

"Twenty years of romance make a woman look like a ruin; but twenty years of marriage make her something like a public building." [Oscar Wilde]

TIP 321 Style: sentence structure tip

One way to make your reader interested enough in your sentences (or sentence fragments) to want to read right through to the end is to make the most interesting word the last one. Use the invaluable device of curiosity. Make the reader want to find out what you're writing about. Don't do this all the time, but, used judiciously, this device can be very effective.

"The more one gets to know of men, the more one values dogs." [A. Toussenel]
You didn't know what the point of this sentence was until the end – and it should have come as a surprise. How much better than:
One values dogs more, as one gets to know more of men.

Another:
"Charity, dear Miss Prism, charity! None of us is perfect. I myself am particularly susceptible to draughts." [Oscar Wilde]

Only when you reach the last word is the point made.

The cleverest writers use this device to end a paragraph, a short story, and even a novel. But, like everything else, don't do it all the time – even if you could!

TIP 322 Style: paragraphs

Paragraphs are built up of sentences. The sections of your work form your paragraphs.
- First write what is often called a key or main sentence, making the main point of what you want to say.
- This sentence sums up what the rest of the paragraph will be about. It's normally, but not always, the first sentence.
- So, it follows that you now make more points about your key sentence. These must be connected with it and follow on naturally from it.
- The look of your paragraphs is important. They should not be too long, as readers often get quickly tired of reading without a break for the eye. I'm sure you've had to plough through very long paragraphs.
- Long paragraphs also impede understanding. Readers need a visual break to think about what you've just told them.
- It may be appropriate to leave a blank line to show that there is a paragraph break.
- However, there may be reasons of space or style why this cannot be done; so indent (type in two or three blank spaces before the first word or leave a small gap at the beginning of the line).

Here is now a paragraph with a key sentence and other sentences following on from this:
English Essentials Explained *was written to instruct and guide anyone from teenager to grandparent who needed help with English grammar. There are sections, dealing with grammar, common errors, punctuation, spelling (including foreign words and phrases),*

style, drafting, writing and proofreading. The sections are designed to work together and to overlap. The series is suitable for those who have little knowledge of the subjects covered; for those who have some gaps in their knowledge; and it could also help those for whom English is a second language.

This is quite long enough for a paragraph.

Note that, on the Internet, paragraphs are often restricted to just two or three sentences. Have a look for yourself and try to work out why.

TIP 323 Style: how to link paragraphs
Try to link your next paragraph to the one before with a word or phrase such as: *also, best of all, even better, here's why, how you will benefit, however, in addition, secondly, so remember, that's why, the result?*

Look at the question. This taps into a basic human instinct, that of curiosity, so this is an excellent way of getting your readers to read on to find the answer.

Remember to use this device of curiosity whenever you can.

TIP 324 Words on words
Twenty five per cent of all written and spoken English is made up of these ten words: *a, and, I, in, is, it, of, that, the, to*

So, I hear you say, I've got 75% of longer words left. Indeed, but remember what you learned above, namely that a shorter word is preferable to a longer one (not a rule I always manage to keep, as you may have noticed). Just think of one reader, someone you know perhaps. Will s/he understand every word? This is how I try to write for you! (And note 'try to' not 'try and' which is heard everywhere and is best avoided except, perhaps, in colloquial speech.)

Although most of your written work should consist of short words, short sentences and short paragraphs, this could become boring, so add variety and sometimes vary the length of any one of these (but not all three at the same time!). A useful tip is to look at a few opening sentences in books, especially novels. Also, observe how the sentence and paragraph lengths vary.

Another tip, explained earlier but worth repeating here, is to count your words. If you're regularly writing sentences containing more than 17-20 words, they are too long. One way of discovering whether your sentence is too long is to read it aloud. If you run out of breath, it's too long! (Just try reading this entire paragraph as though it were one long sentence and you'll see what I mean!) Split the sentences up if necessary. Use a few more full stops.

TIP 325 Style: checklist
As you write, keep the following in mind. Return to this list often to make sure you're keeping to the 'rules'. Check that you have:

- Used a short word rather than a long one where there is a choice.
- Not been long-winded.
- Not used too many adjectives.
- Not used clichés.
- Constructed paragraphs correctly.
- Not repeated yourself.
- Not used tautology (saying the same thing more than once, e.g. *I, myself, personally*).
- Not used jargon, technical words, foreign words or flowery phrases. If you use any of these, make sure they are absolutely necessary.
- Not been inconsistent, e.g. *ice cream, icecream, ice-cream*. Decide which you prefer and stick to it.
- Constructed your sentences properly; made them varied in length, and varied between simple; compound; and complex. (Note: as a general rule, and for training your style, avoid complex sentences if you can use a simple or a compound sentence.)
- Used short sentences with some variety of pace if you can.
- Not taken too long to get to the point.
- Not told your reader but *shown* him/her.
- Avoided starting sentences with the rather tame 'there' or 'it':
  It was a cold day… ✗
  The day was cold… ✓
- Used the active rather than the passive (see Unit 1). Your spellchecker may well know this one. Consider changing if you're reminded. However, you may decide that the passive is best in certain circumstances.
  The boy threw the ball (active). ✓
  The ball was thrown by the boy (passive). ✗
- Made your writing interesting enough for your reader. Of course, if you haven't, s/he is likely to stop reading.
- Made your writing sound sincere. Sincerity follows, provided that you have been clear, brief, committed etc. without special effort.
- Made your style pleasant and elegant. This may be more difficult at first. Try reading it aloud. It's important that people should enjoy reading what you've written. Of course, in any type of fiction, this is essential. If you write as if you were speaking, your style will be easy, natural and a pleasure for your reader.
- Made your spelling, grammar and punctuation correct. You'll know by now, I'm sure, that you can't write anything unless all these are in place. If you're still unsure, ask advice from someone you know who has an excellent command of English grammar etc. It's no use asking someone who is *not* an expert to advise you. It won't help.
- Not written whole sentences or paragraphs that add nothing and should be deleted.

To sum up. Have you:
- used short words, short sentences and short paragraphs?
- been precise and not vague?
- written in the shortest way that is effective for your purpose?
- put the right words in the right places?

All this will come much easier with practice. Think back to something you thought was difficult, but now you find easy, like cooking a meal, driving a car or using the Internet.

Try writing something every day, even a diary or a few paragraphs in a notebook on anything you like, as long as it has:
- **CORRECT WORDS**
- **CORRECT SENTENCES**
- **CORRECT PARAGRAPHS**

TIP 326 Literary terms
This is a personal choice from a large number. The majority of these are called 'figures of speech'. Unless you need to know the names of these for any reason, don't feel you have to learn all these terms. **Don't confuse figures of speech and parts of speech (nouns, verbs, adjectives, adverbs etc.).**

Figures of speech add colour, interest and fun to writing. When I was at university, one of my favourite English classes was called Rhetoric. This was where, on one memorable day, we had to write down 179 figures of speech, most with difficult Greek names. At the end of the hour, the lecturer stated that the last one was 'myxomatosis' – you may recognise his witty reference to a disease of rabbits!

You'll know some of the following, and will most certainly use them, as it's unlikely any of us gets through a day without so doing. Like every other stylistic device, however, use the following sparingly and only when your point is best made that way.

TIP 327 Alliteration
You may remember this one: it's the same sound several times in succession.

Look at these: *Peter Piper picked a peck of pickled pepper… "In a somer seson, whan softe was the sonne…"* [William Langland] I'm sure you can understand this 14th-century English poet. The title of this book: *English Essentials Explained*.

TIP 328 Climax
This is normally three statements, each increasing in intensity. (The word comes from the Greek for 'ladder'. You may remember what Julius Caesar said as he concluded one of his major campaigns in Gaul: *"Veni, vidi, vinci."* ("I came, I saw, I conquered.")

TIP 329 Euphemism
If you don't want to use the 'proper' word for something, you may find yourself using a euphemism. This may be because a word (or few words) would not be acceptable to you, or to your listener or reader.

Going to the bathroom, not making it through an operation, passing away, friendly fire, downsizing etc. are all euphemisms, where, for different reasons, the more straightforward, unpleasant, embarrassing or offensive words are not chosen.

TIP 330 Hyperbole

Hyperbole (pronounced 'hypérbolee') is deliberately exaggerating what is said or written, usually in order to impress the reader or listener: *I drank gallons of water in the swimming pool. "Ten thousand saw I at a glance…"* [William Wordsworth]
The cake was as big as a mountain.

Note that the last example is simultaneously an example of hyperbole and of simile.

TIP 331 Irony and sarcasm

1. **Irony** is usually subtle, and can be amusing and witty. Those in the know are fully aware of the double meaning of the words spoken or written, and realise that the opposite of the words is the truth: *What a pleasant personality he has* (when he hasn't). *How well you play the violin* (when you don't). *"For Brutus is an honourable man …"* (when he wasn't). [William Shakespeare]

2. **Sarcasm** is an unkind, cutting remark, often using irony: *"Lord Birkenhead is very clever, but sometimes his brains go to his head."* [Margot Asquith]
"Lillian Gish may be a charming person, but she is not Ophelia. She comes on stage as if she had been sent for to sew rings on the new curtains." [Mrs. Patrick Campbell]

Don't use either of these too often when writing – or speaking!

TIP 332 Malapropism

Because English has so many words that sound the same, it's easy to use what is called a malapropism, namely using one word for another, and thinking it is right. This is named after the character, Mrs Malaprop, from Richard Brinsley Sheridan's *The Rivals*. In this play, she made such pronouncements as:
She's as headstrong as an allegory on the banks of the Nile.

A more modern example: *She said that she was going to bear* (for 'bare') *her soul and tell everyone some very personal stories about her life.*

You're likely to notice others saying malapropisms. Often it's wiser to keep silent at this point!

TIP 333 Meiosis or litotes

This is the opposite of hyperbole, so the opposite of exaggeration (under-stating). It's not used often: *"Congratulations on your Oscar." "It was nothing." It was not a very calm sea* (when it was extremely rough).

TIP 334 Metaphor

We use metaphors all the time: the head of an organisation, the arm of a chair, an icon on your desktop etc. All these and more have other more literal meanings.

A metaphor is similar to a simile, but a metaphor states that one thing *is* another rather than stating it's *like* another: *One man's meat is another man's poison. "I have no relish for the country; it is a kind of healthy grave."* [Sydney Smith] *She dropped a brick.*

Mixed metaphors occur when two or more metaphors are used together. The resulting sentence often ties your brain into knots: *Because it was raining cats and dogs, he had to pull in his horns.* *"Egghead weds hourglass."* [Anonymous, on the marriage of Arthur Miller and Marilyn Monroe]

And, if you really want to know, there are extended metaphors, such as: *"Our bodies are our gardens, to which our wills are gardeners. We plant flowers and weeds, which are pruned by our consciences."* [Anonymous]

TIP 335 Metonymy
This is where something closely associated is used instead of the actual thing: *The kettle's boiling.* (Used instead of saying that the water is boiling.)

TIP 336 Onomatopoeia
(Pronounced 'onomatopéea'; adjective: onomatopoeic) The sound of the words echoes their sense: *splash, sizzle, buzz, clatter, crunch, squelch, swish, babble, cuckoo, croak* *"The moan of doves in immemorial elms, And murmuring of innumerable bees."* [Alfred, Lord Tennyson]

TIP 337 Paradox
A paradox is a seemingly absurd contraction. When a paradox is used, you have to think of the underlying meaning – not always easy: *Poor little rich girl, clean dirt,* *"The Child is father of the Man…"* [William Wordsworth]

TIP 338 Personification
This a) gives feelings or attributes to non-human things and b) makes an abstract noun into a person: *The stream chattered across the rocks. Death stalks its victims. Hope took her by the hand* (also alliteration).

TIP 339 Pathetic fallacy
This is an extension of personification (TIP 338). Human feelings are attributed to nature: *The sun raged down on the refugees all day. "The stars will awaken Though the moon sleep a full hour later."* [Percy Bysshe Shelley]

TIP 340 Pun
A pun is the humorous use of a word to suggest different meanings; or words of the same sound but with different meanings. The spelling of the two words may vary. It's often described as a play on words.

Puns are frequently used in newspaper headlines. They are used particularly in funny or light writing: *"Diplomacy – lying in state."* [Oliver Herford] *"It is very vulgar to talk like a dentist when one isn't a dentist. It produces a false impression."* [Oscar Wilde]

I must share with you my favourite pun, taken from William Shakespeare's Sonnet 104: *"To me, fair friend, you never can be old,* *For as you were when first your eye I eyed,* *Such seems your beauty still…."*

But, remember, if your pun is tasteless, leave it out.

TIP 341 Rhetorical question
This device is one used regularly and to great effect by most public speakers. This is a question that is posed, but not answered. It has, as you might expect, a question mark. The listener supplies his/her own answer: *"What music is more enchanting than the voices of young people, when you can't hear what they say?"* [Logan Pearsall Smith] *"What is the use of a book,"* thought Alice, *"without pictures or conversations?"* [Lewis Carroll] *How do you do?*

TIP 342 Simile
A simile (pronounced 'similee') is when two things are compared, using 'like' or 'as': *"The photographer is like the cod which produces a million eggs in order that one may reach maturity."* [George Bernard Shaw]
"He was like a cock who thought the sun had risen to hear him crow." [George Eliot]
He was as thin as a rake; she was as white as a sheet (and many other similar similes).

Note how effective the simile can often be for saying something unpleasant!

The plural of this word is 'similes' (pronounced 'similees').

TIP 343 Solecism
(Pronounced 'solesism'.) This is the ignorant use of case, gender or tense, and is what is being committed every time any of the mistakes described in *English Essentials Explained* occurs: *Them be the books I want. If I had worked harder, I* may *have got a better job. Between you and* I, *the truth is never likely to be known.*

Put these right!

TIP 344 Spoonerism
An Oxford cleric, the Rev. W. A. Spooner, was reputed to have made errors such as the following, in his speech. Note how, by transposing the first letters (or the first syllables), the mistake is made: *"To our queer old dean." She hissed the mystery lecture.*

Spoonerisms can be used to comic effect – but use sparingly.

TIP 345 Synecdoche
(Pronounced 'sinécdokey'.) Here, a part is used instead of the whole, or vice versa, the whole for the part (examples in this order): *All hands on deck* (closely followed by the rest of the body?), *England beat Spain at football.*

TIP 346 Tautology
Tautology is saying the same thing twice: *close confidant, exactly pinpoint, free gift, pan fried* (where else would you fry?), *PIN* (Personal Identification Number) *number, train station* (station = a regular stopping place on a railway line), *two twins*

Just omit the tautological part of each word group.

TIP 347 Transferred epithet

Here the adjective (epithet) is moved from the person or thing it describes to another person or thing: *"The dog sniffed the wet-nosed pavement."* [Dylan Thomas]
She worked all day at her weary computer.

Not one you're likely to use, but you may hear the term.

TIP 348 Zeugma

(Pronounced 'zyougma'.) This is where you link two ideas, often one abstract and one concrete with the same verb (the term means 'yoke'):
He lost his dog and his temper. She ate the cake and her words.

TIP 349 Drafting, writing and proofreading

Now it's time to look more closely at how to write. If you take this stage by stage, you'll find it a lot easier than you might have imagined.

I strongly advise against writing without any preparation or revision.

1. First, think about what you have to say or write; perhaps make some notes on paper or in a computer document (the latter is much easier for revising your work). Don't try to put your thoughts in order at this stage. If you have too much material, this can be pruned later. Brainstorm everything to do with the subject without stopping to think too hard.
2. Now read these jottings through and delete those that now seem irrelevant or repetitious.
3. Group words, points or sentences together on the same topic or part of the topic.
4. Try to put these groups in order of importance (you can always change this later).
5. This may be the time to write your introduction and conclusion, but, again, either or both can be left until later if you wish.
6. Write the first draft from the material you have prepared, as above. Don't worry too much about the accuracy of the grammar, punctuation and spelling at this point.
7. Think about the best words to use to convey your intention (use an online thesaurus to help).
8. Now look critically at your first draft. Where are you fairly satisfied? Which parts need more attention? Think about the reader/listener all the time.
9. Make notes all over your work, or add and delete on your computer. It should look a mess at this stage, on paper at least.
10. Try reading it aloud. Where does it flow easily and where is it not so effective? Improve where necessary. Is the meaning clear?
11. Have you left anything out? Said something twice or three times?
12. Write it again, checking the register (TIPs 308-313) and paying more attention to grammar, spelling and punctuation.
13. First write your document; and then spellcheck it. Look out for the common errors: 'whose' for 'who's', 'their' for 'there', which your spellchecker could miss.
14. Check the common typos: 'you' for 'your'; 'form' for 'from'; 'to' for 'too'; 'on' for 'in'; and any you know that you sometimes make.

15. Print it out. Check it again for errors. Ideally leave it for a few hours or longer. Check it again. Improve it.

16. Check the paragraphs. Does each one seamlessly follow on from the last? Are they different lengths? They probably should be. (If in doubt, shorter is usually better than longer.)

17. Look particularly at your opening sentence and your opening paragraph. Unless obliged to do so, your reader may not get past the first sentence if this does not entice her or him into the rest of the first paragraph. Remember curiosity: this is a good device for your first sentence – make the reader want to find out what happens next. You need to spend a long time on the first sentence and the first paragraph: they are the most important of the whole piece of writing.

18. And the last paragraph: does that go out with a bang or a whimper? Apart from the first sentence, the last one is the most important.

19. Are there any paragraphs which add little or nothing and which could be omitted? Making someone read more than is necessary will not help the overall effect of your work.

20. Check the subject you have been given again. Have you written what is required or have you wandered from the point?

21. You may note that I didn't mention a title (if required) for your work. This is because I didn't want you to waste time at the beginning thinking of a title, as this will evolve as you work. Indeed, it may change several times, as has the title for the work you're now reading. *English Essentials Explained* has had at least three working titles.

22. Now start thinking about the length. If you've been given a precise length, how much shorter or longer is your second draft? Add or subtract words or paragraphs where necessary. Hint: use the word-counting facility on your computer if you have one. If no length is stipulated, do you think you've written about the right amount?

23. Now write/type out what could be your final draft. At this stage, you must ensure that spelling, grammar and punctuation are as nearly perfect as you can make them. If you're not sure of a word, substitute another: the English language has many ways of saying the same thing.

24. If it's not too long, read your work aloud, word by word, sentence by sentence, paragraph by paragraph. Check particularly words/grammar etc. that you know you're weak in (e.g. writing sentences or paragraphs which are too long). Go through this draft with just that in mind. You need to read once for the flow and possibly more than once concentrating on the essentials of grammar, punctuation, spelling etc.

25. Read it through again. Is it good enough? If not, do it again and again, until you're satisfied that this is the best you can possibly make it. After all, sometimes a great deal depends on just one piece of work. (As an example, what you're now reading plus the other Units took many months, many drafts and much revising and rewriting before I was [almost] satisfied with it. And even now, it's very unlikely to be entirely error-free, but one has to stop some time!)

26. Finally, if possible, leave your work after you think it's as good as you can make it and come back to it hours or a day or two later. You're almost guaranteed to improve it if you do this.

27. If you can, ask someone else to look at it for you – I did, and many suggestions were made as a result. Some I accepted, but other times I was happy to leave what I had written.

28. Revision can take as long or even longer than the first draft. But this stage should not be skipped. Learn to be a perfectionist!

29. And finally, just before you print or send off your finely honed piece of work, spellcheck it one last time. You might just be surprised by the odd spelling error or extra space that has crept in unnoticed. I always am!

Note

If you ever have to fill in a form by hand (e.g. an application form for a job) which has paragraphs of words, photocopy or scan the blank form first. Write the details on the photocopy or scan in pencil, so that you can make alterations. Use the original copy only when you're quite sure you're satisfied with your answers.

A clean, smooth and neatly written form gives a much better impression of you than a crumpled messy one with alterations.

Unit 5: Review

Answer the questions. Answers on Pages 158-159.

1. What is the rule with acronyms?
2. What are these examples of? *Dog for sale: eats anything and is fond of children. Crossbred horses.*
3. Why might you be in trouble if you called your hero 'Hals Masters'?
4. These are words you should avoid: 'cherry pick', 'quality time', 'feel good factor', 'meltdown'. What are they examples of?
5. A colon can be used to sum up what you've just said. Where does it go here? *I got up early, made the breakfast, took the children to school, cleaned the house, did the ironing in short, a tiring morning.*
6. Is this sentence acceptable? *And so they went home.*
7. What is an idiom?
8. *To really get where you want to go.* What is this an example of?
9. I saw 'Slope Remediation' near some roadworks. What did it mean? Merely that a sloping part of an exit road was being repaired! This is an example of what?
10. Why is this poor style? 1 of the 3 decided to leave.
11. What is a paraphrase?
12. What is a summary?
13. Which 'person' is normally used when writing novels?
14. Which register do these words fall into? *Freebie, stuff, er, sort of, you know.*

15. Rewrite this more formally: *What time will he get there?*
16. Which type of English should you use in formal writing?
17. Write down the five most important rules for clarity of style. 1.
18. 2.
19. 3.
20. 4.
21. 5.
22. What three questions do you ask yourself to select the right style? 1.
23. 2.
24. 3.
25. Should you write shorter or longer words?
26. Should you use simpler or more complex words?
27. What's wrong with using 'get', 'nice' and similar everyday words?
28. What is the stylistic advantage of putting the most important word at the end of a sentence?
29. What is the most important part of a paragraph?
30. What makes one paragraph flow smoothly into the next?
31. What is the maximum number of words you should write in a sentence?
32. What are the three main building blocks that are required for anything you write?
33. This is an example of which figure of speech? *She sells seashells on the seashore.*
34. What are these examples of? 'Discomfort' for 'pain'; 'vertically challenged' for 'short'.
35. What is hyperbole?
36. *"Have a good day," I said to a neighbour putting in a new window in pouring rain.* Which figure of speech?
37. *Low and behold. From time memorial.* Which figure of speech?
38. Which figure of speech is the opposite of hyperbole?
39. *She was an angel.* Which figure of speech?
40. Define onomatopoeia.
41. A paradox is an apparent what?
42. *The wind smiled as it ruffled her hair.* Which figure of speech?
43. *I love this ship: she glides so smoothly over the water.* This is?
44. *Speak up! I can't hear: I've got aids in both ears.* Which figure of speech?
45. *Have you got nothing better to do?* Which figure of speech?
46. *She was like an angel.* Which figure of speech?
47. *The bum of the flightlebee.* Which figure of speech?
48. *Put your best foot forward.* Which figure of speech?
49. Tautology is when you...?
50. Zeugma does what?

Unit 1: Answers

The number in square brackets at the end of each answer refers to the relevant Tip(s).

1. Eight [1]
2. Definite [3]
3. An [4]
4. The name of a person, place or thing [5]
5. Proper [6]
6. Abstract [7]
7. Collective [8]
8. One which can be counted, e.g. day [9]
9. No [11]
10. A word ending, such as –ness [12]
11. It says what someone or something is doing or is. [14]
12. Past, present, future [16, 3 marks] [15]
13. Regular [17]
14. Irregular [17]
15. Main [18]
16. to be, to have, to do [19, 3 marks]
17. Question tag [22]
18. To show future time [23]
19. No, it should be 'may'. [27]
20. No, it should be 'If he could eat less…'. [28]
21. The person or thing that does or is the verb. [29]
22. This is the person or thing being or doing the verb. [31]
23. A new set of rules is… [31]
24. Subject, verb, object [32, 3 marks]
25. clothes, shoes, suitcase [33, 3 marks]
26. Intransitive [34]
27. A verb of state/feeling [36]
28. We [37]
29. Infinitives [38]
30. Active [40]
31. *If I were you* [41]
32. Present participles [42]
33. No [44]
34. *She said, 'Can you come?'* [44]
35. No. *Either John or Patrick has to drive.* [45]
36. Yes [46]
37. To qualify a noun [47]
38. In front of a noun or after a verb [48, 2 marks]
39. Yes [47]
40. *a large bright pink furry toy* [49, 2 marks or 1 for a near miss]

41. *She wanted a large, bright pink, furry toy.* [49]
42. Positive, comparative, superlative [51, 3 marks]
43. big, bigger, biggest [51]
44. good, better, best [52]
45. No, it should be *I do like those kinds of books.* [53]
46. Possessive [54]
47. No, 'For every...' [55]
48. Yes [57]
49. No. 'The girl was happier...' [61]
50. How, when or where the action of the verb happened or was [60, 3 marks]
51. badly, worse, worst [62]
52. No. 'However, the train...' [63]
53. Adverbs [65]
54. No. *Drive carefully.* [66]
55. A word used instead of a noun [68]
56. I, she, they, etc. [68]
57. No. '...by him and me' [68]
58. Yes [73]
59. *Everyone waited her* or *her/his* or *his/her turn.* [74]
60. It joins words or other constructions. [76]
61. and, but [76, 2 marks]
62. A word or group of words placed in front of a noun or pronoun [77]
63. A word expressing surprise or some other feeling. *Help!* [80, 2 marks]
64. It is poor style. [80]
65. It is a group of words which makes complete sense. It begins with a capital letter and ends with a full stop. [81]
66. One with a subject, a verb and an object, e.g. *I love you.* [81, 3 marks]
67. One, e.g. *Jump!* [81]
68. statement, question, command, exclamation [82, 4 marks]
69. One with just one main clause [83]
70. A clause which depends on the main clause – it is not a sentence. [84]
71. Compound [85]
72. One with a main clause plus one or more subordinate/dependent clauses [86]
73. *I have been writing this list of questions for two hours now. It is very difficult, especially as I want to test you before and after you have studied the grammar concerned and I don't want to make the questions too difficult or too easy. I hope that I have succeeded and that the marks add up to 100.* [88, up to 4 marks]
74. No. *I don't want to write any more sentences.* [89]
75. A group of words which does not express a complete thought. *On a train* [90, 2 marks]

N.B. The information over the page is identical for Unit 2.

Don't ever let a good score make you complacent. Always think before you speak or write: this will make such a difference to the impression you give of yourself to others.

81-100 This is an excellent score. All you have to do is to brush up on the ones you got wrong. Give yourself a pat on the back, and go out into the world feeling confident that your English is very unlikely to let you down – because you think before you speak or write. Congratulations!

61-80 You've done well; and you have a good command of English. However, there are still gaps to be filled. Look at the points you got wrong and decide whether it was lack of thought or lack of knowledge that caused the errors. Rectify these, and you'll be fine.

41-60 Still some way to go before you can be sure you're not making mistakes. Make the effort to learn those points you don't yet know, and then have another go at the questions. You can do it!

21-40 Your English may let you down at some point if this is your score. It's vital that you go through the whole course carefully, paying particular attention to points you found difficult to answer.

1-20 English of this standard is bound to let you down at some point. Go through the whole course slowly, not moving from TIP to TIP until you've mastered each one.

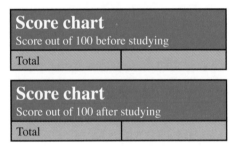

Score chart	
Score out of 100 before studying	
Total	

Score chart	
Score out of 100 after studying	
Total	

Unit 2: Answers

1. Advanced [92]
2. Advice [93]
3. Affected [94]
4. Enabled [97]
5. Allowed [98]
6. A lot [99]
7. All ready [100]
8. All right [101]
9. Altogether [103]
10. Always/all ways [104]
11. Among [105]
12. Immoral [106]
13. Number [107]
14. Any more [109]
15. Anyone [110]
16. Any time [111]
17. Any way [112]
18. Our/are [114]
19. Insure [115]
20. Prevent [116]
21. Badly [117]
22. That [118]
23. Me [120]
24. Bored [122]
25. Break [123]
26. Breathe [125]
27. Buy/by [126]
28. Castor [128]
29. Childish [130]
30. Classic [132]
31. Course [133]
32. With [134]
33. Complimented [135]
34. Continuously [137]

35. Current [138]
36. Defective [139]
37. Dependent [141]
38. Dessert [142]
39. Dyed [143]
40. Direct [145]
41. Uninterested [146]
42. Edible [149]
43. Economical [150]
44. i.e. [151]
45. e.g. [151]
46. Elicit [152]
47. Enormity [155]
48. etc. [157]
49. Every day [158]
50. Every one [159]
51. Fewer [161]
52. For ever [162]
53. Formerly [163]
54. Historic [165]
55. Me [166]
56. Implied [167]
57. Initiated [169]
58. Into [170]
59. It's [171]
60. Only [172]
61. Lie [174]
62. Led [175]
63. Let's [176]
64. Slander [177]
65. As if [178]
66. Lose [180]
67. Might [181]
68. May be [182]

69. Moral [183]
70. No one [184]
71. On to [185]
72. Overlook [186]
73. Passed [187]
74. Practice [189]
75. Principle [190]
76. Proceeded [191]
77. Provided [193]
78. Quiet [194]
79. Raise [195]
80. Role [197]
81. Sitting [198]
82. Sheer [199]
83. Sight [201]
84. Soul [202]
85. Stationary [204]
86. Standing [205]
87. They're [210]
88. There are [211]
89. Theirs [212]
90. Those sorts [213]
91. Tied [214]
92. Too [215]
93. Told [216]
94. Waived [219]
95. Wonder [220]
96. Whether/weather [221]
97. Where/were [222]
98. Whose [224]
99. Women [225]
100. You're [226]

Score chart
Score out of 100 before studying

Total	

Score chart
Score out of 100 after studying

Total	

Unit 3: Answers

1. *Tim and James decided to cross the Atlantic in a small boat.* [227]
2. *I decided to study Russian, French and Latin.* [228]
3. *We saw 'Romeo and Juliet' last Wednesday.* [228]
4. *Did you see the film last night?* [229]
5. Full stop [230]
6. Lack of thought, carelessness [234]
7. When the question is implied, in indirect speech [236]
8. To divide up sentences to make them more easily understood [241]
9. *The large parcel, Michael, is for you.* [244]
10. *The work, up to now, has not been too difficult.* [245]
11. *Also, there are two more advantages.* [246]
12. Yes. *If you can't finish it today, do it tomorrow.* [248]
13. *She loved Denmark; it was her favourite country.* [250]
14. No. *One of the best-loved actors visited our town.* [251]
15. *I wanted to get home early, so I worked very quickly.* [253]
16. 12,345,678 [254]
17. Stronger [256]
18. To unite sentences that are closely associated [257]
19. *Summer is hot; by contrast, winter is cold.* [257]
20. To expand in the second half of a sentence what is in the first half [260]
21. *I wanted to buy another car: mine was very old.* [260]
22. *I won't do any more.* [262]
23. No. *You're too late.* [263]
24. *They're not coming.* [263]
25. *I should have known.* Careless muddling between 'have' and 'of' [263]
26. *Someone's broken my pen.* [263]
27. No. *My uncle's house was near ours.* [264]
28. No. *bottles and jars* [267]
29. *'Susie, I do very much appreciate your help,' she said.* [268]
30. *'Clean your shoes,' she shouted, 'and brush your teeth!'* [268]
31. No [270]
32. *If you like (and you don't have to), you can go tomorrow.* [271]
33. A dash separates words, but a hyphen links them. [272]
34. *We decided to have a picnic – it was a hot day.* [272]
35. *A three-legged dog; an ugly-looking building; sixty-four* [273]
36. Three dots showing something has been left out or the sentence could continue... [274]
37. Because this is lazy. It is not a substitute for other punctuation marks. [274]
38. Check that all bullet points follow the same grammatical pattern. [275]
39. For emphasis and for foreign words [276]
40. It marks a division of words or lines. [277]

41. to 50. Give yourself the mark you think you deserve out of 10 for the following paragraph. Here is one way of doing it:

Oh yes, I know what it's like to be frightened. I remember once, when I was about twelve years old, I was left in the house. It was near Christmas, and the weather was cold and damp. That didn't matter too much though, as we had an open fire with hot coals. I had been left in charge of my younger brother David and my sister Caroline. This wasn't the first time; in fact, it happened often. David and Caroline were arguing as usual, and David pushed Caroline too close to the fire. There was a guard, but it was loose, and Caroline knocked it to one side. She fell towards the hot flames! What was I to do?

N.B. The information below is identical for Units 3, 4 and 5.

41-50 This is an excellent score. All you have to do is to brush up on the ones you got wrong. Give yourself a pat on the back, and go out into the world feeling confident that your English is very unlikely to let you down – because you think before you speak or write. Congratulations!

31-40 You've done well; and you have a good command of English. However, there are still gaps to be filled. Look at the points you got wrong and decide whether it was lack of thought or lack of knowledge that caused the errors. Rectify these, and you'll be fine.

21-30 Still some way to go before you can be sure you're not making mistakes. Make the effort to learn those points you don't yet know, and then have another go at the questions. You can do it!

11-20 Your English may let you down at some point if this is your score. It's vital that you go through the whole course carefully, paying particular attention to points you found difficult to answer.

0-10 English of this standard is bound to let you down at some point. Go through the whole course slowly, not moving from TIP to TIP until you've mastered each one.

Score chart
Score out of 50 before studying

Total	

Score chart
Score out of 50 after studying

Total	

Unit 4: Answers

1. using [279]
2. argument [279]
3. referred [280]
4. planning [280]
5. stories [281]
6. paid [281]
7. accessible [282]
8. responsible [282]
9. disappeared [283]
10. dissimilar [283]
11. mislaid [284]
12. missold [284]
13. mosquitoes [285]
14. solos [285]
15. believe [286]
16. seized [286]
17. mischievous [286]
18. advice [287]
19. exercise [287]

See Common misspellings [TIP 288] These are the correct spellings:
20. accommodation
21. broccoli
22. calendar
23. definitely
24. embarrassing
25. hygiene
26. government
27. immediately
28. liaison
29. misspell
30. occasionally
31. particularly
32. responsibility
33. secretary
34. unnecessary

See Foreign words, Foreign phrases and Abbreviations [TIPs 289-291]
35. appendices
36. bacterium
37. Italian
38. Medicine without any drugs
39. Where bus or train stops
40. Each dish priced separately

41. Office to exchange currencies
42. Gambling
43. Restaurant
44. An author
45. Time flies
46. Before noon
47. e.g.
48. And the rest, et cetera
49. Note well
50. At the end of a letter

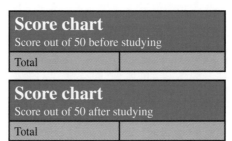

Score chart
Score out of 50 before studying

Total	

Score chart
Score out of 50 after studying

Total	

Unit 5: Answers

1. Write the words in full the first time; use the shortened words thereafter. [292]
2. Ambiguity [293]
3. Problems may occur when you need a second 's': Hals's, Masters's [295]
4. Cliché [296]
5. *I got up early, made the breakfast, took the children to school, cleaned the house, did the ironing: in short, a tiring morning.* [297]
6. Yes, it is acceptable to begin a sentence with 'and' where appropriate. [299]
7. A group of words whose meaning cannot be understood from just the individual words [301]
8. Split infinitive [302]
9. Jargon [303]
10. A number as the first word of a sentence should be written as a word in formal English. Numbers up to ten are often written as words. [304]
11. A version of similar length to the original text in your own words [305]
12. A shortened version of the original text [305]
13. Third [306]
14. Very informal language or slang [309]
15. What time will he arrive? [310]
16. Standard English [313]
17. Clear thoughts [315]
18. Get to the point quickly. [315]
19. Write simply. [315]
20. Make a list of the main points. [315]
21. Subdivide into paragraphs and put in order of importance. [315]
22. Why am I writing? [316]
23. Who am I writing for? [316]
24. Where will this be read? [316]
25. Shorter [317]
26. Simpler [317]
27. They are overused words: there is usually a better alternative, especially when writing formally. [319]
28. It uses the device of curiosity, and ensures the reader will read through to the end of the sentence. [321]
29. The main or key sentence, often the first [322]
30. Linking words or phrases [323]
31. 17-20 [324]
32. Words, sentences, paragraphs [325]
33. Alliteration [327]
34. Euphemism [329]
35. A deliberate exaggeration [330]
36. Irony [331]
37. Malapropism [332]
38. Meiosis or litotes [333]
39. Metaphor [334]

40. The sound of the words echoes the sense. [336]
41. Contradiction [337]
42. Pathetic fallacy [338]
43. Personification [339]
44. Pun [340]
45. Rhetorical question [341]
46. Simile [342]
47. Spoonerism [344]
48. Synecdoche [345]
49. Say the same thing twice [346]
50. Joins two ideas with one verb [348]

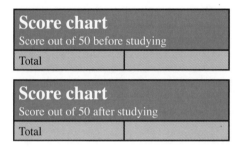

Score chart	
Score out of 50 before studying	
Total	

Score chart	
Score out of 50 after studying	
Total	

Total scores: units 1 to 5

Score chart	
Score out of 350 before studying	
Total	

Score chart	
Score out of 350 after studying	
Total	

Bibliography

Austin, T, THE TIMES Guide to English Style and Usage, London, The Times, 1998

Bryson, B, Troublesome Words, London, Penguin, 2009

Burchfield, R.W. (ed.), The New Fowler's Modern English Usage, Oxford University Press, 1996

Burt, A, Quick Solutions to Common Errors in English, Oxford, how to books, 2009

Chalker, S, English Grammar Word by Word, Walton-on-Thames, Nelson, 1990

Crystal, D, The Cambridge Encyclopedia of the English Language, Cambridge University Press, 1995

Fergusson, R, Cassell's Dictionary of English Idioms, Cambridge, Cassell, 2002

Gowers, Sir E, The Complete Plain Words, London, Penguin, 2004

Parrish, T, The Grouchy Grammarian, New Jersey, BCA, 2002

Partridge, E, Usage and Abusage, Harmondsworth, Penguin, 2005

Roget, P, Thesaurus, London, Penguin, 2004 (I was fascinated to find Roget's grave in the churchyard next to the last school I taught in – I often went there to say thank you!)

Room, A, Cassell's Foreign Words and Phrases, London, Cassell, 2002

Sherrin, N, The Oxford Dictionary of Humorous Quotations, Oxford University Press, 2009

Swan, M, and Walker, C, How English Works, Oxford University Press, 1997

Swan, M, Practical English Usage, Oxford University Press, 2005 (This was written for students for whom English is a second language and, as such, explains everything very clearly.)

The Concise Oxford Dictionary, Oxford University Press, 2009 (I use this if I don't feel like struggling with the bigger **Shorter**.)

The Oxford Dictionary of Quotations, Oxford University Press, 2009

The Oxford Manual of Style, Oxford University Press, 2003

The Shorter Oxford English Dictionary, Oxford University Press, 2007 (This isn't shorter – it's in two large volumes. I bought mine in 1974 and have used it regularly ever since.)